By the same author

THE JOHANNINE GOSPEL IN GNOSTIC EXEGESIS
PAUL THE GNOSTIC: GNOSTIC EXEGESIS
OF THE PAULINE LETTERS

THE
GNOSTIC
GOSPELS

THE GNOSTIC GOSPELS

by ELAINE PAGELS

RANDOM HOUSE

New York

Library of Congress Cataloging in Publication Data

Pagels, Elaine H 1943–
The gnostic Gospels.

Includes index.
1. Gnosticism. 2. Chenoboskion manuscripts.
I. Title.
BT1390.P3   273'1   79–4764
ISBN 0–394–50278–7

Designed by Anita Karl

Manufactured in the United States of America

6 7 8 9

To Elizabeth Diggs and Sharon Olds
in loving friendship

ACKNOWLEDGMENTS

T HE WRITING of this book began several years ago with research into the relation between politics and religion in the origins of Christianity. The first four chapters have been published in more technical form in scholarly journals (specific references precede the footnotes of each chapter).

In preparing this volume I have generally chosen to follow the translations offered in *The Nag Hammadi Library*, edited by James M. Robinson, since these are readily available to all readers. In certain cases, however, I have changed the translation for the sake of clarity, consistency or interpretation (for example, I have translated the Coptic transliteration of the Greek term τελείωσις not as "perfection," but as "fulfillment," which seems to me more accurate; in other cases, where the Coptic term πρωμε apparently translates the Greek ἄνθρωπος, I have translated it not as "man" but as "humanity"). In the case of two texts, I have used different translations (see below).

I am especially grateful to those colleagues and friends who have read and criticized the entire manuscript: Peter Berger, John Gager, Dennis Groh, Howard Kee, George MacRae, Wayne Meeks and Morton Smith. For other advice and criticism, specifically of aspects of the introduction, I owe grateful thanks to Marilyn Harran, Marvin Meyer, Birger Pearson, Gilles

Acknowledgments

Quispel, Richard Ogust and James M. Robinson. I am grateful, too, to Bentley Layton for permission to use his translation of the *Treatise on Resurrection*, and to James Brashler for permission to use his translation of the *Apocalypse of Peter*.

Special thanks are due the Rockefeller Foundation, the Lita A. Hazen Foundation and the Guggenheim Foundation for their support, which granted me the time to devote to writing; and to President Jacqueline Mattfeld and Vice President Charles Olton for approving a year's leave from my responsibilities at Barnard College. Especially I wish to thank Lydia Bronte and Lita A. Hazen for their encouragement throughout the whole project.

The present version of the book would have been impossible to produce without the superb editing of Jason Epstein, Vice President and Editorial Director of Random House; the excellent advice of John Brockman; and the conscientious work of Connie Budelis in typing and Barbara Willson in copyediting.

Finally, I wish to thank my husband for his loving encouragement in the process of this work.

CONTENTS

INTRODUCTION

I N DECEMBER 1945 an Arab peasant made an astonishing
archeological discovery in Upper Egypt. Rumors obscured
the circumstances of this find—perhaps because the discovery
was accidental, and its sale on the black market illegal. For years
even the identity of the discoverer remained unknown. One
rumor held that he was a blood avenger; another, that he had
made the find near the town of Naj 'Hammādī at the Jabal
al-Ṭārif, a mountain honeycombed with more than 150 caves.
Originally natural, some of these caves were cut and painted and
used as grave sites as early as the sixth dynasty, some 4,300 years
ago.

Thirty years later the discoverer himself, Muḥammad 'Alī
al-Sammān, told what happened.[1] Shortly before he and his
brothers avenged their father's murder in a blood feud, they had
saddled their camels and gone out to the Jabal to dig for *sabakh*,
a soft soil they used to fertilize their crops. Digging around a
massive boulder, they hit a red earthenware jar, almost a meter
high. Muḥammad 'Alī hesitated to break the jar, considering that
a *jinn*, or spirit, might live inside. But realizing that it might also
contain gold, he raised his mattock, smashed the jar, and discovered inside thirteen papyrus books, bound in leather. Return-
ing to his home in al-Qaṣr, Muḥammad 'Alī dumped the books

and loose papyrus leaves on the straw piled on the ground next to the oven. Muḥammad's mother, 'Umm-Aḥmad, admits that she burned much of the papyrus in the oven along with the straw she used to kindle the fire.

A few weeks later, as Muḥammad 'Alī tells it, he and his brothers avenged their father's death by murdering Ahmed Ismā'īl. Their mother had warned her sons to keep their mattocks sharp: when they learned that their father's enemy was nearby, the brothers seized the opportunity, "hacked off his limbs . . . ripped out his heart, and devoured it among them, as the ultimate act of blood revenge."[2]

Fearing that the police investigating the murder would search his house and discover the books, Muḥammad 'Alī asked the priest, al-Qummuṣ Bāsīlīyuṣ Abd al-Masīḥ, to keep one or more for him. During the time that Muḥammad 'Alī and his brothers were being interrogated for murder, Rāghib, a local history teacher, had seen one of the books, and suspected that it had value. Having received one from al-Qummus Bāsīlīyūs, Rāghib sent it to a friend in Cairo to find out its worth.

Sold on the black market through antiquities dealers in Cairo, the manuscripts soon attracted the attention of officials of the Egyptian government. Through circumstances of high drama, as we shall see, they bought one and confiscated ten and a half of the thirteen leather-bound books, called codices, and deposited them in the Coptic Museum in Cairo. But a large part of the thirteenth codex, containing five extraordinary texts, was smuggled out of Egypt and offered for sale in America. Word of this codex soon reached Professor Gilles Quispel, distinguished historian of religion at Utrecht, in the Netherlands. Excited by the discovery, Quispel urged the Jung Foundation in Zürich to buy the codex. But discovering, when he succeeded, that some pages were missing, he flew to Egypt in the spring of 1955 to try to find them in the Coptic Museum. Arriving in Cairo, he went at once to the Coptic Museum, borrowed photographs of some of the texts, and hurried back to his hotel to decipher them. Tracing out the first line, Quispel was startled, then in-

credulous, to read: "These are the secret words which the living
Jesus spoke, and which the twin, Judas Thomas, wrote down."³
Quispel knew that his colleague H.-C. Puech, using notes from
another French scholar, Jean Doresse, had identified the opening
lines with fragments of a Greek *Gospel of Thomas* discovered
in the 1890's. But the discovery of the whole text raised new
questions: Did Jesus have a twin brother, as this text implies?
Could the text be an authentic record of Jesus' sayings? According to its title, it contained the *Gospel According to Thomas*;
yet, unlike the gospels of the New Testament, this text identified
itself as a *secret* gospel. Quispel also discovered that it contained
many sayings known from the New Testament; but these sayings, placed in unfamiliar contexts, suggested other dimensions
of meaning. Other passages, Quispel found, differed entirely
from any known Christian tradition: the "living Jesus," for
example, speaks in sayings as cryptic and compelling as Zen
koans:

> Jesus said, "If you bring forth what is within you, what
> you bring forth will save you. If you do not bring forth
> what is within you, what you do not bring forth will destroy
> you."⁴

What Quispel held in his hand, the *Gospel of Thomas*, was only
one of the fifty-two texts discovered at Nag Hammadi (the
usual English transliteration of the town's name). Bound into the
same volume with it is the *Gospel of Philip*, which attributes to
Jesus acts and sayings quite different from those in the New
Testament:

> . . . the companion of the [Savior is] Mary Magdalene.
> [But Christ loved] her more than [all] the disciples, and
> used to kiss her [often] on her [mouth]. The rest of [the
> disciples were offended] . . . They said to him, "Why do you
> love her more than all of us?" The Savior answered and said
> to them, "Why do I not love you as (I love) her?"⁵

Other sayings in this collection criticize common Christian
beliefs, such as the virgin birth or the bodily resurrection, as

naïve misunderstandings. Bound together with these gospels is the *Apocryphon* (literally, "secret book") *of John*, which opens with an offer to reveal "the mysteries [and the] things hidden in silence" which Jesus taught to his disciple John.[6]

Muḥammad 'Alī later admitted that some of the texts were lost—burned up or thrown away. But what remains is astonishing: some fifty-two texts from the early centuries of the Christian era—including a collection of early Christian gospels, previously unknown. Besides the *Gospel of Thomas* and the *Gospel of Philip*, the find included the *Gospel of Truth* and the *Gospel to the Egyptians*, which identifies itself as "the [sacred book] of the Great Invisible [Spirit]."[7] Another group of texts consists of writings attributed to Jesus' followers, such as the *Secret Book of James*, the *Apocalypse of Paul*, the *Letter of Peter to Philip*, and the *Apocalypse of Peter*.

What Muhammad 'Alī discovered at Nag Hammadi, it soon became clear, were Coptic translations, made about 1,500 years ago, of still more ancient manuscripts. The originals themselves had been written in Greek, the language of the New Testament: as Doresse, Puech, and Quispel had recognized, part of one of them had been discovered by archeologists about fifty years earlier, when they found a few fragments of the original Greek version of the *Gospel of Thomas*.[8]

About the dating of the manuscripts themselves there is little debate. Examination of the datable papyrus used to thicken the leather bindings, and of the Coptic script, place them c. A.D. 350–400.[9] But scholars sharply disagree about the dating of the original texts. Some of them can hardly be later than c. A.D. 120–150, since Irenaeus, the orthodox Bishop of Lyons, writing c. 180, declares that heretics "boast that they possess more gospels than there really are,"[10] and complains that in his time such writings already have won wide circulation—from Gaul through Rome, Greece, and Asia Minor.

Quispel and his collaborators, who first published the *Gospel of Thomas*, suggested the date of c. A.D. 140 for the original.[11] Some reasoned that since these gospels were heretical, they must have been written later than the gospels of the New Testament, which are dated c. 60–110. But recently Professor Helmut Koester of Harvard University has suggested that the collection of sayings in the *Gospel of Thomas*, although compiled c. 140, may include some traditions even *older* than the gospels of the New Testament, "possibly as early as the second half of the first century" (50–100)—as early as, or earlier, than Mark, Matthew, Luke, and John.[12]

Scholars investigating the Nag Hammadi find discovered that some of the texts tell the origin of the human race in terms very different from the usual reading of Genesis: the *Testimony of Truth*, for example, tells the story of the Garden of Eden from the viewpoint of the serpent! Here the serpent, long known to appear in gnostic literature as the principle of divine wisdom, convinces Adam and Eve to partake of knowledge while "the Lord" threatens them with death, trying jealously to prevent them from attaining knowledge, and expelling them from Paradise when they achieve it.[13] Another text, mysteriously entitled the *Thunder, Perfect Mind*, offers an extraordinary poem spoken in the voice of a feminine divine power:

> For I am the first and the last.
> I am the honored one and the scorned one.
> I am the whore and the holy one.
> I am the wife and the virgin. . . .
> I am the barren one,
>   and many are her sons. . . .
> I am the silence that is incomprehensible . . .
> I am the utterance of my name.[14]

These diverse texts range, then, from secret gospels, poems, and quasi-philosophic descriptions of the origin of the universe, to myths, magic, and instructions for mystical practice.

WHY WERE THESE TEXTS BURIED—and why have they remained virtually unknown for nearly 2,000 years? Their suppression as banned documents, and their burial on the cliff at Nag Hammadi, it turns out, were both part of a struggle critical for the formation of early Christianity. The Nag Hammadi texts, and others like them, which circulated at the beginning of the Christian era, were denounced as heresy by orthodox Christians in the middle of the second century. We have long known that many early followers of Christ were condemned by other Christians as heretics, but nearly all we knew about them came from what their opponents wrote attacking them. Bishop Irenaeus, who supervised the church in Lyons, c. 180, wrote five volumes, entitled *The Destruction and Overthrow of Falsely So-called Knowledge*, which begin with his promise to

> set forth the views of those who are now teaching heresy
> . . . to show how absurd and inconsistent with the truth are
> their statements . . . I do this so that . . . you may urge all
> those with whom you are connected to avoid such an abyss
> of madness and of blasphemy against Christ.[15]

He denounces as especially "full of blasphemy" a famous gospel called the *Gospel of Truth*.[16] Is Irenaeus referring to the same *Gospel of Truth* discovered at Nag Hammadi? Quispel and his collaborators, who first published the *Gospel of Truth*, argued that he is; one of their critics maintains that the opening line (which begins "The gospel of truth") is not a title.[17] But Irenaeus does use the same source as at least one of the texts discovered at Nag Hammadi—the *Apocryphon* (Secret Book) *of John*—as ammunition for his own attack on such "heresy." Fifty years later Hippolytus, a teacher in Rome, wrote another massive *Refutation of All Heresies* to "expose and refute the wicked blasphemy of the heretics."[18]

This campaign against heresy involved an involuntary admission of its persuasive power; yet the bishops prevailed. By the time of the Emperor Constantine's conversion, when Christianity became an officially approved religion in the fourth century, Christian bishops, previously victimized by the police, now commanded them. Possession of books denounced as heretical was made a criminal offense. Copies of such books were burned and destroyed. But in Upper Egypt, someone, possibly a monk from a nearby monastery of St. Pachomius,[19] took the banned books and hid them from destruction—in the jar where they remained buried for almost 1,600 years.

But those who wrote and circulated these texts did not regard *themselves* as "heretics." Most of the writings use Christian terminology, unmistakably related to a Jewish heritage. Many claim to offer traditions about Jesus that are secret, hidden from "the many" who constitute what, in the second century, came to be called the "catholic church." These Christians are now called gnostics, from the Greek word *gnosis*, usually translated as "knowledge." For as those who claim to know nothing about ultimate reality are called agnostic (literally, "not-knowing"), the person who does claim to know such things is called gnostic ("knowing"). But *gnosis* is not primarily rational knowledge. The Greek language distinguishes between scientific or reflective knowledge ("He knows mathematics") and knowing through observation or experience ("He knows me"), which is *gnosis*. As the gnostics use the term, we could translate it as "insight," for *gnosis* involves an intuitive process of knowing oneself. And to know oneself, they claimed, is to know human nature and human destiny. According to the gnostic teacher Theodotus, writing in Asia Minor (c. 140–160), the gnostic is one who has come to understand

> who we were, and what we have become; where we were
> . . . whither we are hastening; from what we are being
> released; what birth is, and what is rebirth.[20]

Yet to know oneself, at the deepest level, is simultaneously to know God; this is the secret of *gnosis*. Another gnostic teacher, Monoimus, says:

> Abandon the search for God and the creation and other
> matters of a similar sort. Look for him by taking yourself
> as the starting point. Learn who it is within you who makes
> everything his own and says, "My God, my mind, my

thought, my soul, my body." Learn the sources of sorrow, joy, love, hate . . . If you carefully investigate these matters you will find him *in yourself*.[21]

What Muḥammad 'Alī discovered at Nag Hammadi is, apparently, a library of writings, almost all of them gnostic. Although they claim to offer secret teaching, many of these texts refer to the Scriptures of the Old Testament, and others to the letters of Paul and the New Testament gospels. Many of them include the same *dramatis personae* as the New Testament—Jesus and his disciples. Yet the differences are striking.

Orthodox Jews and Christians insist that a chasm separates humanity from its creator: God is wholly other. But some of the gnostics who wrote these gospels contradict this: self-knowledge is knowledge of God; the self and the divine are identical.

Second, the "living Jesus" of these texts speaks of illusion and enlightenment, not of sin and repentance, like the Jesus of the New Testament. Instead of coming to save us from sin, he comes as a guide who opens access to spiritual understanding. But when the disciple attains enlightenment, Jesus no longer serves as his spiritual master: the two have become equal—even identical.

Third, orthodox Christians believe that Jesus is Lord and Son of God in a unique way: he remains forever distinct from the rest of humanity whom he came to save. Yet the gnostic *Gospel of Thomas* relates that as soon as Thomas recognizes him, Jesus says to Thomas that they have both received their being from the same source:

> Jesus said, "I am not your master. Because you have drunk, you have become drunk from the bubbling stream which I have measured out. . . . He who will drink from my mouth will become as I am: I myself shall become he, and the things that are hidden will be revealed to him."[22]

Does not such teaching—the identity of the divine and human, the concern with illusion and enlightenment, the founder who is presented not as Lord, but as spiritual guide—sound more Eastern than Western? Some scholars have suggested that if the names were changed, the "living Buddha" appropriately could say what the *Gospel of Thomas* attributes to the living Jesus. Could Hindu or Buddhist tradition have influenced gnosticism?

The British scholar of Buddhism, Edward Conze, suggests that it had. He points out that "Buddhists were in contact with the Thomas Christians (that is, Christians who knew and used such writings as the *Gospel of Thomas*) in South India."[23] Trade routes between the Greco-Roman world and the Far East were opening up at the time when gnosticism flourished (A.D. 80–200); for generations, Buddhist missionaries had been proselytizing in Alexandria. We note, too, that Hippolytus, who was a Greek-speaking Christian in Rome (c. 225), knows of the Indian Brahmins—and includes their tradition among the sources of heresy:

> There is . . . among the Indians a heresy of those who philosophize among the Brahmins, who live a self-sufficient life, abstaining from (eating) living creatures and all cooked food . . . They say that God is light, not like the light one sees, nor like the sun nor fire, but to them God is discourse, not that which finds expression in articulate sounds, but that of knowledge (*gnosis*) through which the secret mysteries of nature are perceived by the wise.[24]

Could the title of the *Gospel of Thomas*—named for the disciple who, tradition tells us, went to India—suggest the influence of Indian tradition?

These hints indicate the possibility, yet our evidence is not conclusive. Since parallel traditions may emerge in different cultures at different times, such ideas could have developed in both places independently.[25] What we call Eastern and Western religions, and tend to regard as separate streams, were not clearly differentiated 2,000 years ago. Research on the Nag Hammadi texts is only beginning: we look forward to the work of scholars who can study these traditions comparatively to discover whether they can, in fact, be traced to Indian sources.

Even so, ideas that we associate with Eastern religions emerged in the first century through the gnostic movement in the West, but they were suppressed and condemned by polemicists like Irenaeus. Yet those who called gnosticism heresy were adopting—consciously or not—the viewpoint of that group of Christians who called themselves orthodox Christians. A heretic may be anyone whose outlook someone else dislikes or denounces. According to tradition, a heretic is one who deviates from the true faith. But what defines that "true faith"? Who calls it that, and for what reasons?

We find this problem familiar in our own experience. The term "Christianity," especially since the Reformation, has covered an astonishing range of groups. Those claiming to represent "true Christianity" in the twentieth century can range from a Catholic cardinal in the Vatican to an African Methodist Episcopal preacher initiating revival in Detroit, a Mormon missionary in Thailand, or the member of a village church on the coast of Greece. Yet Catholics, Protestants, and Orthodox agree that such diversity is a recent—and deplorable—development. According to Christian legend, the early church was different. Christians of every persuasion look back to the primitive church to find a simpler, purer form of Christian faith. In the apostles' time, all members of the Christian community shared their money and property; all believed the same teaching, and worshiped together; all revered the authority of the apostles. It was only after that golden age that conflict, then heresy emerged: so says the author of the Acts of the Apostles, who identifies himself as the first historian of Christianity.

But the discoveries at Nag Hammadi have upset this picture. If we admit that some of these fifty-two texts represent early forms of Christian teaching, we may have to recognize that early Christianity is far more diverse than nearly anyone expected before the Nag Hammadi discoveries.[26]

Contemporary Christianity, diverse and complex as we find it, actually may show more unanimity than the Christian churches of the first and second centuries. For nearly all Christians since that time, Catholics, Protestants, or Orthodox, have shared three basic premises. First, they accept the canon of the New Testament; second, they confess the apostolic creed; and third, they affirm specific forms of church institution. But every one of these—the canon of Scripture, the creed, and the institutional structure—emerged in its present form only toward the end of the second century. Before that time, as Irenaeus and others attest, numerous gospels circulated among various Christian groups, ranging from those of the New Testament, Matthew, Mark, Luke, and John, to such writings as the *Gospel of Thomas*, the *Gospel of Philip*, and the *Gospel of Truth*, as well as many other secret teachings, myths, and poems attributed to Jesus or his disciples. Some of these, apparently, were discovered at Nag Hammadi; many others are lost to us. Those who identified themselves as Christians entertained many—and radically differing—religious beliefs and practices. And the communities scattered throughout the known world organized themselves in ways that differed widely from one group to another.

Yet by A.D. 200, the situation had changed. Christianity had become an institution headed by a three-rank hierarchy of bishops, priests, and deacons, who understood themselves to be the guardians of the only "true faith." The majority of churches, among which the church of Rome took a leading role, rejected all other viewpoints as heresy. Deploring the diversity of the earlier movement, Bishop Irenaeus and his followers insisted that there could be only one church, and outside of that church, he declared, "there is no salvation."[27] Members of this church alone are orthodox (literally, "straight-thinking") Christians. And, he claimed, this church must be *catholic*—that is, universal. Whoever challenged that consensus, arguing instead for other forms of Christian teaching, was declared to be a heretic, and expelled. When the orthodox gained military support, sometime after the Emperor Constantine became Christian in the fourth century, the penalty for heresy escalated.

. . .

The efforts of the majority to destroy every trace of heretical "blasphemy" proved so successful that, until the discoveries at Nag Hammadi, nearly all our information concerning alternative forms of early Christianity came from the massive orthodox attacks upon them. Although gnosticism is perhaps the earliest—and most threatening—of the heresies, scholars had known only a handful of original gnostic texts, none published before the nineteenth century. The first emerged in 1769, when a Scottish tourist named James Bruce bought a Coptic manuscript near Thebes (modern Luxor) in Upper Egypt.[28] Published only in 1892, it claims to record conversations of Jesus with his disciples—a group that here includes both men and women. In 1773 a collector found in a London bookshop an ancient text, also in Coptic, that contained a dialogue on "mysteries" between Jesus and his disciples.[29] In 1896 a German Egyptologist, alerted by the previous publications, bought in Cairo a manuscript that, to his amazement, contained the *Gospel of Mary* (Magdalene) and three other texts. Three copies of one of them, the *Apocryphon* (Secret Book) *of John* were also included among the gnostic library discovered at Nag Hammadi fifty years later.[30]

But why is this astonishing discovery at Nag Hammadi only now becoming known for the first time? Why did we not hear news of the Nag Hammadi discovery, as we did about the Dead Sea Scrolls, some twenty-five years ago? Professor Hans Jonas, the eminent authority on gnosticism, wrote in 1962:

> Unlike the Dead Sea finds of the same years, the gnostic find from Nag Hammadi has been beset from the beginning to this day by a persistent curse of political roadblocks, litigations, and, most of all, scholarly jealousies and "first-manship" (the last factor has grown by now into a veritable *chronique scandaleuse* of contemporary academia).[31]

Access to the texts was deliberately suppressed not only in ancient times but, for very different reasons, in the more than thirty years since the discovery.[32] In the first place, villagers from Upper Egypt and the antiquities dealers who were trying to get rich from the manuscripts hid them to avoid confiscation by government authorities. Their value became clear when the French Egyptologist Jean Doresse saw the first of the recovered manuscripts in 1947 at the Coptic Museum in Cairo. When the museum's director, Togo Mina, asked him to examine it, Doresse identified the manuscript and announced that this discovery would mark an epoch in the study of the origins of Christianity. Fired by his enthusiasm, Mina asked him to look at another manuscript, held by Albert Eid, a Belgian antiquities dealer in Cairo. Following this meeting, Mina went to see Eid to tell him that he would never allow the manuscript to leave Egypt—it must be sold, for a nominal price, to the museum.

But still the majority of the find remained hidden. Bahīj 'Alī, a one-eyed outlaw from al-Qaṣr, had acquired possession of many of the codices in Nag Hammadi and went to Cairo to sell them. Phōcion Tano, an antiquities dealer, bought all that he had, and went to Nag Hammadi to see if he could find more. While Doresse worked in Cairo through the air raids and bombings of 1948 to publish the manuscript of Codex III, the Minister of Public Education negotiated to buy Tano's collection for the museum. Tano worked fast to prevent the government from interfering, by saying that they belonged to a private party, a woman named Dattari, an Italian collector living in Cairo. But on June 10, 1949, Miss Dattari was unsettled to read the following report in Cairo's French newspaper:

> The acquisition of these precious documents by the Egyptian government is in process. According to the specialists consulted, it has to do with one of the most extraordinary discoveries preserved until the present by the ground of Egypt, surpassing in scientific interest such spectacular discoveries as the tomb of Tutankhamen.[33]

When the government nationalized the collection in 1952, government officials claimed the codices, packed in a sealed suitcase. They paid Miss Dattari nothing—although her asking price had been about £100,000. When she retaliated with a lawsuit, she succeeded only in delaying research for three years by gaining a court injunction against it; she lost the case.

But the government failed to confiscate Eid's part of Codex I. In 1949 Albert Eid, worried about government intervention, flew from Cairo to America. By including the manuscript in a large collection of export items, he succeeded in smuggling it out of Egypt. He offered it to buyers for as much as $22,000, but since at least one prospective buyer refused, fearing that the Egyptian government would resent the sale, he returned disappointed to Belgium, where he placed it in a safe-deposit box protected by a secret password.

The Egyptian government indicted Eid for smuggling antiquities, but by the time of his conviction, the antiquities dealer had died. The court imposed a fine of £6,000 on his estate. Meanwhile Eid's widow secretly negotiated to sell the codex, perhaps even to competing bidders. Professor Gilles Quispel, who urged the Jung Foundation in Zürich to buy it, says he did not know that the export and sale were illegal when he made the arrangements. He enjoys telling the dramatic story of his coup:

> On the 10th day of May, 1952, a professor from Utrecht took a train to Brussels. However, due to his absentmindedness, he stepped out of the train in Tilborg, while thinking he was in Roosendaal, and thus missed his connecting train. But when he finally approached the appointed meeting place, a café somewhere in Brussels, two hours too late, he saw the middleman, from Saint Idesbald close by Coxye on the Belgium coast, still waiting at the window and kindly waving to him. The professor then reached out and handed the man a check for 35,000 Frs.S. In return, the man gave the professor about 50 papyri. How does one manage to transfer them over the border without complications? One cannot very easily hide such a package. Thus one must remain honest, and when the customs official asks, "What do you have in that package?" then one just tells the truth: "An old manuscript." And the customs official makes a gesture of

total disinterest and lets one pass. So this is how the Jung Codex was purchased.[34]

Once ownership of the manuscripts was established by 1952 —twelve and a half codices in the Coptic Museum in Cairo, and most of the thirteenth in a safe-deposit box in Zürich—the texts became, for the next twenty years, the focus of intense personal rivalries among the international group of scholars competing for access to them.

Dr. Pahor Labib, who took over directorship of the Coptic Museum in 1952, decided to keep strict control over publication rights. Publishing the definitive first edition of any one of these extraordinary, original texts—let alone the whole collection— would establish a scholar's reputation internationally. The few to whom Dr. Labib did grant access to the manuscripts protected their interests by refusing to allow anyone else to see them. In 1961 the Director General of UNESCO, alerted to the discovery by French scholars, urged publication of the whole find and proposed setting up an international committee to arrange it.[35] The Scandinavian archeologist Torgny Säve-Söderberg wrote to UNESCO, speaking for himself and other scholars, urging UNESCO to intervene, and to prepare a complete edition of photographs of all the manuscripts in order to place the whole of the discovery at the disposal of the many scholars throughout the world who were impatient to see them.

Ten years later, in 1972, the first volume of the photographic edition finally appeared. Nine other volumes followed between 1972 and 1977, thus putting all thirteen codices in the public domain. Since undertaking such a major technical project in Egypt involved many delays, Professor James Robinson, director of the Institute for Antiquity and Christianity, the only American member of the UNESCO committee, had organized an international team to copy and translate most of the material. Robinson and his team privately circulated this material to scholars throughout the world, thus involving many people in the research, effectively breaking the monopoly that had controlled the discovery.

Introduction

I first learned of the Nag Hammadi discoveries in 1965, when I entered the graduate program at Harvard University to study the history of Christianity. I was fascinated to hear of the find, and delighted in 1968 when Professor George MacRae of Harvard received the mimeographed transcriptions from Robinson's team. Because the official publications had not yet appeared, each page was stamped with a warning:

> This material is for private study by assigned individuals only. Neither the text nor its translation may be reproduced or published in any form, in whole or in part.

MacRae and his colleague Professor Helmut Koester encouraged their students to learn Coptic in order to begin research on this extraordinary find. Convinced that the discovery would revolutionize the traditional understanding of the origins of Christianity, I wrote my dissertation at Harvard and Oxford on the controversy between gnostic and orthodox Christianity. After receiving the Ph.D. from Harvard in 1970 and accepting a faculty position at Barnard College, Columbia University, I worked almost exclusively on early Christian gnosticism. After publishing two technical books on this research,[36] I received grants in 1975 (from the American Council of Learned Societies and the American Philosophical Society) so that I could study the manuscripts at the Cairo Museum and attend the First International Conference on Coptic Studies in Cairo. There, like other scholars, I was initiated to the Coptic Museum, amazed to find the library that houses the manuscripts to be a single, small room of the Coptic Museum. Every day, while children played in the library and cleaning women washed the floor around me, I worked at the table, transcribing the papyri. Having seen only black-and-white photographs, I found the originals surprisingly beautiful—each mounted in plexiglass, inscribed in black ink on golden brown leaves. At the First International Conference, held in Cairo while I was there, I delivered a paper on one of the manuscripts (the *Dialogue of the Savior*),[37] and even met one of the middlemen from al-Qaṣr who sold the texts illegally in Cairo.

Having joined the team of scholars, I participated in preparing the first complete edition in English, published in the United States by Harper & Row in 1977. Only with that publication, and with the completion of the photographic edition expected by 1980, have we finally overcome the obstacles to public knowledge caused by what Professor Gérard Garitte of Louvain called "personal rivalries and . . . pretensions to monopolize documents that belong only to science, that is to say, to all."[38]

BY THE TIME I LEARNED of the discovery, however, gnosticism had already had become the focus of a remarkable amount of research. The first to investigate the gnostics were their orthodox contemporaries. Attempting to prove that gnosticism was essentially non-Christian, they traced its origins to Greek philosophy, astrology, mystery religions, magic, and even Indian sources. Often they emphasized—and satirized—the bizarre elements that appear in some forms of gnostic mythology. Tertullian ridiculed the gnostics for creating elaborate cosmologies, with multi-storied heavens like apartment houses, "with room piled on room, and assigned to each god by just as many stairways as there were heresies: The universe has been turned into rooms for rent!"[39] By the end of the nineteenth century, when the few original gnostic sources noted above were discovered, they inspired new research among scholars. The great German historian Adolf von Harnack, basing his research primarily on the church fathers, regarded gnosticism as a Christian heresy. Writing in 1894, Harnack explained that the gnostics, interpreting Christian doctrine in terms of Greek philosophy, became, in one sense, the "first Christian theologians."[40] But in the process, he contended, they distorted the Christian message, and propagated false, hybrid forms of Christian teaching—what

[xxix]

he called the "acute Hellenizing of Christianity."[41] The British scholar Arthur Darby Nock agreed: gnosticism, he said, was a kind of "Platonism run wild."[42]

Other historians of religion objected. Far from being a Christian heresy, they said, gnosticism originally was an independent religious movement. In the early twentieth century the New Testament scholar Wilhelm Bousset, who traced gnosticism to ancient Babylonian and Persian sources, declared that

> gnosticism is first of all a pre-Christian movement which had roots in itself. It is therefore to be understood . . . in its own terms, and not as an offshoot or byproduct of the Christian religion.[43]

On this point the philologist Richard Reitzenstein agreed; but Reitzenstein went on to argue that gnosticism derived from ancient Iranian religion and was influenced by Zoroastrian traditions.[44] Others, including Professor M. Friedländer, maintained that gnosticism originated in Judaism: the heretics whom the rabbis attacked in the first and second centuries, said Friedländer, were Jewish gnostics.[45]

In 1934—more than ten years before the Nag Hammadi discoveries—two important new books appeared. Professor Hans Jonas, turning from the question of the historical sources of gnosticism, asked where it originated *existentially*. Jonas suggested that gnosticism emerged in a certain "attitude toward existence." He pointed out that the political apathy and cultural stagnation of the Eastern empire in the first two centuries of this era coincided with the influx of Oriental religion into Hellenistic culture. According to Jonas' analysis, many people at the time felt profoundly alienated from the world in which they lived, and longed for a miraculous salvation as an escape from the constraints of political and social existence. Using the few sources available to him with penetrating insight, Jonas reconstructed a gnostic world view—a philosophy of pessimism about the world combined with an attempt at self-transcendence.[46] A nontechnical version of his book, translated into English, remains, even today, the classic introduction.[47] In an epilogue added to the second edition of this book, Jonas drew a parallel between gnosticism and twentieth-century existentialism, acknowledging his debt to existentialist philosophers, especially to Heidegger, in forming his interpretation of "the gnostic religion."[48]

Another scholar, Walter Bauer, published a very different view of gnosticism in 1934. Bauer recognized that the early Christian movement was itself far more diverse than orthodox sources chose to indicate. So, Bauer wrote,

> perhaps—I repeat, perhaps—certain manifestations of Christian life that the authors of the church renounce as "heresies" originally had not been such at all, but, at least here and there, were the only forms of the new religion; that is, for those regions, they were simply "Christianity." The possibility also exists that their adherents . . . looked down with hatred and scorn on the orthodox, who for them were the false believers.[49]

Bauer's critics, notably the British scholars H. E. W. Turner[50] and C. H. Roberts,[51] have criticized him for oversimplifying the situation and for overlooking evidence that did not fit his theory. Certainly Bauer's suggestion that, in certain Christian groups, those later called "heretics" formed the majority, goes beyond even the gnostics' own claims: they typically characterized themselves as "the few" in relation to "the many" (*hoi polloi*). But Bauer, like Jonas, opened up new ways of thinking about gnosticism.

The discoveries at Nag Hammadi in 1945 initiated, as Doresse had foreseen, a whole new epoch of research. The first and most important task was to preserve, edit, and publish the texts themselves. An international team of scholars, including Professors A. Guillaumont and H.-Ch. Puech from France, G. Quispel from the Netherlands, W. Till from Germany, and Y. ʿAbd al Masīḥ from Egypt, collaborated in publishing the *Gospel of Thomas* in 1959.[52] Many of the same scholars worked with Professors M. Malinine of France, R. Kasser of Germany, J. Zandee of the Netherlands, and R. McL. Wilson of Scotland to edit the texts from Codex I. Professor James M. Robinson, secretary of the International Committee for the Nag Hammadi Codices, organized a team of scholars from Europe, Canada, and the United States to edit the facsimile edition of photographs[53] as well as a complete scholarly edition of the whole find in Coptic and English. Robinson sent copies of manuscripts and translations to colleagues in Berlin. There, members of the *Berliner Arbeitskreis für koptisch-gnostische Schriften* (Berlin Working-Group for Coptic-Gnostic Texts), a circle that includes such eminent scholars as Professors H. M. Schenke, K. M. Fischer, and K. W. Tröger, and collaborates with others, including E. Haenchen, W. Schmithals, and K. Rudolf, has prepared editions of the texts in Coptic and German, as well as numerous commentaries, books, and articles.

What could this wealth of new material tell us about gnosticism? The abundance of the texts—and their diversity— made generalization difficult, and consensus even more difficult. Acknowledging this, most scholars now agree that what we call "gnosticism" was a widespread movement that derived its sources from various traditions. A few of the texts describe the multiple heavens, with magic passwords for each one, that the church fathers who had criticized gnosticism led scholars to expect; but many others, surprisingly, contain nothing of the kind. Much of the literature discovered at Nag Hammadi is distinctively Christian; some texts, however, show little or no Christian influence; a few derive primarily from pagan sources (and may not be "gnostic" at all); others make extensive use of Jewish traditions. For this reason, the German scholar C. Colpe has challenged the historians' search for the "origins of gnosticism."[54] This method, Colpe insists, leads to a potentially infinite regress of ever remoter "origins" without contributing much to our understanding of what gnosticism actually is.

Recently several scholars have sought the impetus for the development of gnosticism not in terms of it cultural origins, but in specific events or experiences. Professor R. M. Grant has suggested that gnosticism emerged as a reaction to the shattering of traditional religious views—Jewish and Christian—after the Romans destroyed Jerusalem in A.D. 70.[55] Quispel proposed that gnosticism originated in a potentially universal "experience of the self" projected into religious mythology.[56] Jonas has offered a typological scheme describing gnosticism as a specific kind of philosophical world view.[57] The British scholar E. R. Dodds characterized gnosticism as a movement whose writings derived from mystical experience.[58] Gershom Scholem, the eminent Professor of Jewish Mysticism at the Hebrew University in Jerusalem, agrees with Dodds that gnosticism involves mystical speculation and practice. Tracing esoteric currents in rabbinic circles that were contemporary with the development of gnosticism, Scholem calls them forms of "Jewish gnosticism."[59]

Today, those investigating the Nag Hammadi texts are less concerned about constructing comprehensive theories than analyzing in detail the sources unearthed at Nag Hammadi. There are several different types of research, each investigating primarily those specific groups of texts appropriate to the purposes of the inquiry. One type of research, concerned with the relationship of gnosticism to Hellenistic philosophy, focuses primarily on those Nag Hammadi texts that exemplify this relationship. Contributors to this aspect of research include, for example (besides Hans Jonas), the British scholars A. D. Nock[60] and A. H. Armstrong,[61] and such American scholars as Professors Bentley Layton[62] of Yale University and Harold Attridge of Southern Methodist University.[63] Professor Morton Smith of Columbia University, on the other hand, whose current research concerns the history of magic, investigates the sources that evince magical practice.[64]

A second direction of research investigates gnostic texts from a literary and form-critical point of view. Much of this work was initiated by J. M. Robinson and H. Koester in their book *Trajectories Through Early Christianity*.[65] Others have explored the rich symbolism of gnostic texts. The French scholar M. Tardieu, for example, has analyzed gnostic myths;[66] Professor L. Schottroff has investigated gnostic accounts of the powers of evil.[67] Many of their American colleagues, too, have contributed to the literary analysis of gnostic sources. Professor P. Perkins has investigated both genre[68] and imagery;[69] Professor George MacRae has contributed to our understandings of gnostic metaphors,[70] myth,[71] and literary form;[72] he and others, including Quispel and Professor B. A. Pearson, have shown how certain gnostic myths drew upon material traditional in Judaism.[73]

A third direction of research (which often overlaps with the second) explores the relation of gnosticism to its contemporary religious environment. While Scholem, MacRae, Quispel, Pearson (to name a few) have demonstrated that some gnostic sources refer extensively to Jewish tradition, others are examining the question: What do the gnostic texts tell us about the origins of Christianity? The many scholars who have shared in this research, besides those mentioned above, include Professors R. M. Grant and E. Yamauchi in the United States; R. McL. Wilson in Scotland; G. C. Stead and H. Chadwick in England; W. C. van Unnik in the Netherlands; H.-Ch. Puech and Dr. S. Petrement in France; A. Orbe in Spain; S. Arai in Japan; J. Ménard and F. Wisse in Canada; and, in Germany, besides the members of the Berliner Arbeitskreis, A. Böhlig and Dr. K. Koschorke. Because my own research falls into this category (i.e., gnosticism and early Christianity), I have selected primarily the gnostic Christian sources as the basis for this book. Rather than considering the question of the origins of gnosticism, I intend here to show how gnostic forms of Christianity interact with orthodoxy—and what this tells us about the origins of Christianity itself.

Given the enormous amount of current research in the field, this sketch is necessarily brief and incomplete. Whoever wants to follow the research in detail will find invaluable help in the *Nag Hammadi Bibliography*, published by Professor D. M. Scholer.[74] Kept up to date by regular supplements published in the journal *Novum Testamentum*, Scholer's bibliography currently lists nearly 4,000 books, editions, articles, and reviews published in the last thirty years concerning research on the Nag Hammadi texts.

Yet even the fifty-two writings discovered at Nag Hammadi offer only a glimpse of the complexity of the early Christian movement. We now begin to see that what we call Christianity —and what we identify as Christian tradition—actually represents only a small selection of specific sources, chosen from among dozens of others. Who made that selection, and for what reasons? Why were these other writings excluded and banned as "heresy"? What made them so dangerous? Now, for the first time, we have the opportunity to find out about the earliest Christian heresy; for the first time, the heretics can speak for themselves.

Gnostic Christians undoubtedly expressed ideas that the orthodox abhored. For example, some of these gnostic texts question whether all suffering, labor, and death derive from human sin, which, in the orthodox version, marred an originally perfect creation. Others speak of the feminine element in the divine, celebrating God as Father *and* Mother. Still others suggest that Christ's resurrection is to be understood symbolically, not literally. A few radical texts even denounce catholic Christians themselves as heretics, who, although they "do not understand mystery . . . boast that the mystery of truth belongs to them alone."[75] Such gnostic ideas fascinated the psychoanalyst C. G. Jung: he thought they expressed "the other side of the mind"—the spontaneous, unconscious thoughts that any orthodoxy requires its adherents to repress.

Yet orthodox Christianity, as the apostolic creed defines it, contains some ideas that many of us today might find even stranger. The creed requires, for example, that Christians confess that God is perfectly good, and still, he created a world that includes pain, injustice, and death; that Jesus of Nazareth was born of a virgin mother; and that, after being executed by order of the Roman procurator, Pontius Pilate, he arose from his grave "on the third day."

Introduction

Why did the consensus of Christian churches not only accept these astonishing views but establish them as the only true form of Christian doctrine? Traditionally, historians have told us that the orthodox objected to gnostic views for religious and philosophic reasons. Certainly they did; yet investigation of the newly discovered gnostic sources suggests another dimension of the controversy. It suggests that these religious debates—questions of the nature of God, or of Christ—simultaneously bear social and political implications that are crucial to the development of Christianity as an institutional religion. In simplest terms, ideas which bear implications contrary to that development come to be labeled as "heresy"; ideas which implicitly support it become "orthodox."

By investigating the texts from Nag Hammadi, together with sources known for well over a thousand years from orthodox tradition, we can see how politics and religion coincide in the development of Christianity. We can see, for example, the *political* implications of such orthodox doctrines as the bodily resurrection—and how gnostic views of resurrection bear opposite implications. In the process, we can gain a startlingly new perspective on the origins of Christianity.

THE
GNOSTIC
GOSPELS

CHAPTER

I

The Controversy over Christ's Resurrection: Historical Event or Symbol?

"JESUS CHRIST ROSE from the grave." With this proclamation, the Christian church began. This may be the fundamental element of Christian faith; certainly it is the most radical. Other religions celebrate cycles of birth and death: Christianity insists that in one unique historical moment, the cycle reversed, and a dead man came back to life! For Jesus' followers this was the turning point in world history, the sign of its coming end. Orthodox Christians since then have confessed in the creed that Jesus of Nazareth, "crucified, dead, and buried," was raised "on the third day."[1] Many today recite that creed without thinking about what they are saying, much less actually believing it. Recently some ministers, theologians, and scholars have challenged the literal view of resurrection. To account for this doctrine, they point out its psychological appeal to our deepest fears and hopes; to explain it, they offer symbolic interpretations.

But much of the early tradition insists literally that a man —Jesus—had come back to life. What makes these Christian accounts so extraordinary is not the claim that his friends had "seen" Jesus after his death—ghost stories, hallucinations, and visions were even more commonplace then than now—but that they saw an actual human being. At first, according to Luke, the disciples themselves, in their astonishment and terror at the appearance of Jesus among them, immediately assumed that they were seeing his ghost. But Jesus challenged them: "Handle me and see, for a spirit does not have flesh and bones, as you see that I have."[2] Since they remained incredulous, he asked for something to eat; as they watched in amazement, he ate a piece of broiled fish. The point is clear: no ghost could do that.

Had they said that Jesus' spirit lived on, surviving bodily decay, their contemporaries might have thought that their stories made sense. Five hundred years before, Socrates' disciples had claimed that their teacher's soul was immortal. But what the Christians said was different, and, in ordinary terms, wholly implausible. The finality of death, which had always been a part of the human experience, was being transformed. Peter contrasts King David, who died and was buried, and whose tomb was well known, with Jesus, who, although killed, rose from the grave, "because it was not possible for him to be held by it"—that is, by death.[3] Luke says that Peter excluded metaphorical interpretation of the event he said he witnessed: "[We] ate and drank with him after he rose from the dead."[4]

Tertullian, a brilliantly talented writer (A.D. c. 190), speaking for the majority, defines the orthodox position: as Christ rose bodily from the grave, so every believer should anticipate the resurrection of the flesh. He leaves no room for doubt. He is not, he says, talking about the immortality of the soul: "The salvation of the soul I believe needs no discussion: for almost all heretics, in whatever way they accept it, at least do not deny it."[5] What is raised is "this flesh, suffused with blood, built up with bones, interwoven with nerves, entwined with veins, (a flesh) which . . . was born, and . . . dies, undoubtedly human."[6] Tertullian expects the idea of Christ's suffering, death, and resurrection to shock his readers; he insists that "it must be believed, because it is absurd!"[7]

Yet some Christians—those he calls heretics—dissent. Without denying the resurrection, they reject the literal interpretation; some find it "extremely revolting, repugnant, and impossible." Gnostic Christians interpret resurrection in various ways. Some say that the person who experiences the resurrection does not meet Jesus raised physically back to life; rather, he encounters Christ on a spiritual level. This may occur in dreams, in ecstatic trance, in visions, or in moments of spiritual illumination. But the orthodox condemn all such interpretations; Tertullian declares that anyone who denies the resurrection *of the flesh* is a heretic, not a Christian.

Why did orthodox tradition adopt the literal view of resurrection? The question becomes even more puzzling when we look at what the New Testament says about it. Some accounts, like the story we noted from Luke, tell how Jesus appears to his disciples in the form they know from his earthly life; he eats with them, and invites them to touch him, to prove that he is "not a ghost." John tells a similar story: Thomas declares that he will not believe that Jesus had actually risen from the grave unless he personally can see and touch him. When Jesus appears, he tells Thomas, "Put your finger here, and see my hands; and put out your hand, and place it in my side; do not be faithless, but believing."[8] But other stories, directly juxtaposed with these, suggest different views of the resurrection. Luke and Mark both relate that Jesus appeared "in another form"[9]—*not* his former earthly form—to two disciples as they walked on the road to Emmaus. Luke says that the disciples, deeply troubled about Jesus' death, talked with the stranger, apparently for several hours. They invited him to dinner; when he sat down with them to bless the bread, suddenly they recognized him as Jesus. At that moment "he vanished out of their sight."[10] John, too, places directly before the story of "doubting Thomas" another of a very different kind: Mary

Magdalene, mourning for Jesus near his grave, sees a man she takes to be the gardener. When he speaks her name, suddenly she recognizes the presence of Jesus—but he orders her *not* to touch him.[11]

So if some of the New Testament stories insist on a literal view of resurrection, others lend themselves to different interpretations. One could suggest that certain people, in moments of great emotional stress, suddenly felt that they experienced Jesus' presence. Paul's experience can be read this way. As he traveled on the Damascus road, intent on arresting Christians, "suddenly a light from heaven flashed about him. And he fell to the ground," hearing the voice of Jesus rebuking him for the intended persecution.[12] One version of this story says, "The men who were traveling with him stood speechless, hearing the voice, but seeing no one";[13] another says the opposite (as Luke tells it, Paul said that "those who were with me saw the light, but did not hear the voice of the one who was speaking to me").[14] Paul himself, of course, later defended the teaching on resurrection as fundamental to Christian faith. But although his discussion often is read as an argument for bodily resurrection, it concludes with the words "I tell you this, brethren: flesh and blood cannot inherit the kingdom of God, nor does the perishable [that is, the mortal body] inherit the imperishable."[15] Paul describes the resurrection as "a mystery,"[16] the transformation from physical to spiritual existence.

If the New Testament accounts could support a range of interpretations, why did orthodox Christians in the second century insist on a literal view of resurrection and reject all others as heretical? I suggest that we cannot answer this question adequately as long as we consider the doctrine only in terms of its religious content. But when we examine its practical effect on the Christian movement, we can see, paradoxically, that the doctrine of bodily resurrection also serves an essential *political* function: it legitimizes the authority of certain men who claim to exercise exclusive leadership over the churches as the successors of the apostle Peter. From the second century, the doctrine has served to validate the apostolic succession of bishops, the basis of papal authority to this day. Gnostic Christians who interpret resurrection in other ways have a lesser claim to authority: when they claim priority over the orthodox, they are denounced as heretics.

Such political and religious authority developed in a most remarkable way. As we have noted, diverse forms of Christianity flourished in the early years of the Christian movement. Hundreds of rival teachers all claimed to teach the "true doctrine of Christ" and denounced one another as frauds. Christians in churches scattered from Asia Minor to Greece, Jerusalem, and Rome split into factions, arguing over church leadership. All claimed to represent "the authentic tradition."

How could Christians resolve such contrary claims? Jesus himself was the only authority they all recognized. Even during his lifetime, among the small group traveling through Palestine with him, no one challenged—and no one matched—the authority of Jesus himself. Independent and assertive a leader as he was, Jesus censured such traits among his followers. Mark relates that when James and John came to him privately to ask for special positions in his administration, he spoke out sharply against their ambition:

> You know that those who are supposed to rule over the Gentiles lord it over them, and their great men exercise authority over them. But it shall not be so among you; but whoever would be great among you must be your servant, and whoever would be first among you must be slave of all.[17]

After Jesus' execution his followers scattered, shaken with grief and terrified for their own lives. Most assumed that their enemies were right—the movement had died with their master. Suddenly, astonishing news electrified the group. Luke says that they heard that "the Lord has risen indeed, and has appeared to Simon [Peter]!"[18] What had he said to Peter? Luke's account suggested to Christians in later generations that he named Peter as his successor, delegating the leadership to him. Matthew says that during his lifetime Jesus already had decided that Peter, the "rock," was to found the future institution.[19] Only John claims to tell what the risen Christ said: he told Peter that he was to take Jesus' place as "shepherd" for the flock.[20]

Whatever the truth of this claim, we can neither verify nor disprove it on historical grounds alone. We have only second-hand testimony from believers who affirm it, and skeptics who deny it. But what we do know as historical fact is that certain disciples—notably, Peter—*claimed* that the resurrection had happened. More important, we know the result: shortly after Jesus' death, Peter took charge of the group as its leader and spokesman. According to John, he had received his authority from the only source the group recognized—from Jesus himself, now speaking from beyond the grave.

What linked the group gathered around Jesus with the world-wide organization that developed within 170 years of his death into a three-rank hierarchy of bishops, priests, and deacons? Christians in later generations maintained that it was the claim that Jesus himself had come back to life! The German scholar Hans von Campenhausen says that because "Peter was the first to whom Jesus appeared after his resurrection,"[21] Peter became the first leader of the Christian community. One can dispute Campenhausen's claim on the basis of New Testament evidence: the gospels of Mark and John both name Mary Magdalene, not Peter, as the first witness of the resurrection.[22] But orthodox churches that trace their origin to Peter developed the tradition —sustained to this day among Catholic and some Protestant churches—that Peter had been the "first witness of the resurrection," and hence the rightful leader of the church. As early as the second century, Christians realized the potential political consequences of having "seen the risen Lord": in Jerusalem, where James, Jesus' brother, successfully rivaled Peter's authority, one tradition maintained that James, not Peter (and certainly not Mary Magdalene) was the "first witness of the resurrection."

New Testament evidence indicates that Jesus appeared to many others besides Peter—Paul says that once he appeared to five hundred people simultaneously. But from the second century, orthodox churches developed the view that only *certain* resurrection appearances actually conferred authority on those who received them. These were Jesus' appearances to Peter and to "the eleven" (the disciples minus Judas Iscariot, who had betrayed Jesus and committed suicide).[23] The orthodox noted the account in Matthew, which tells how the resurrected Jesus announced to "the eleven" that his own authority now has reached cosmic proportions: "All authority, on heaven and on earth, has been given to me." Then he delegated that authority to "the eleven disciples."[24] Luke, too, indicates that although many others had known Jesus, and even had witnessed his resurrection, "the eleven" alone held the position of *official* witnesses—and hence became official leaders of the whole community. Luke relates that Peter, acting as spokesman for the group, proposed that since Judas Iscariot had defected, a twelfth man should now "take the office" that he vacated, restoring the group as "the twelve."[25] But to receive a share in the disciples' authority, Peter declared that he must be

> one of the men who have accompanied us during all the time that the Lord Jesus went in and out among us, beginning from the baptism of John until the day he was taken up from us—*one of these men must become with us a witness to his resurrection.*[26]

Matthias, who met these qualifications, was selected and "enrolled with the eleven apostles."[27]

After forty days, having completed the transfer of power, the resurrected Lord abruptly withdrew his bodily presence from them, and ascended into heaven as they watched in amazement.[28] Luke, who tells the story, sees this as a momentous event. Henceforth, for the duration of the world, no one would ever experience Christ's actual presence as the twelve disciples had during his lifetime—and for forty days after his death. After that time, as Luke tells it, others received only less direct forms of communication with Christ. Luke admits that Stephen saw a vision of Jesus "standing at the right hand of God";[29] that Paul first encountered Jesus in a dramatic vision, and later in a trance[30] (Luke claims to record his words: "When I had returned to Jerusalem and was praying in the temple, I fell into a trance and saw him speaking to me"[31]). Yet Luke's account implies that these incidents cannot compare with the original events attested by the Twelve. In the first place, they occurred to persons *not* included among the Twelve. Second, they occurred only *after* Jesus' bodily ascension to heaven. Third, although visions, dreams, and ecstatic trances manifested traces of Christ's spiritual presence, the experience of the Twelve differed entirely. They alone, having known Jesus throughout his lifetime, could testify to those unique events which they knew firsthand—and to the resurrection of one who was dead to his complete, physical presence with them.[32]

Whatever we think of the historicity of the orthodox account, we can admire its ingenuity. For this theory—that all authority derives from certain apostles' experience of the resurrected Christ, an experience now closed forever—bears enormous implications for the political structure of the community. First, as the German scholar Karl Holl has pointed out, it restricts the circle of leadership to a small band of persons whose members stand in a position of incontestable authority.[33] Second, it suggests that only the apostles had the right to ordain future leaders as their successors.[34] Christians in the second century used Luke's account to set the groundwork for establishing specific, restricted chains of command for all future generations of Christians. Any potential leader of the community would have to derive, or claim to derive, authority from the same apostles. Yet, according to the orthodox view, none can ever claim to equal their authority—much less challenge it. What the apostles experienced and attested their successors cannot verify for themselves; instead, they must only believe, protect, and hand down to future generations the apostles' testimony.[35]

This theory gained extraordinary success: for nearly 2,000 years, orthodox Christians have accepted the view that the apostles alone held definitive religious authority, and that their only legitimate heirs are priests and bishops, who trace their ordination back to that same apostolic succession. Even today the pope traces his—and the primacy he claims over the rest—to Peter himself, "first of the apostles," since he was "first witness of the resurrection."

But the gnostic Christians rejected Luke's theory. Some gnostics called the literal view of resurrection the "faith of fools."[36] The resurrection, they insisted, was not a unique event in the past: instead, it symbolized how Christ's presence could be experienced in the present. What mattered was not literal seeing, but spiritual vision.[37] They pointed out that many who witnessed the events of Jesus' life remained blind to their meaning. The disciples themselves often misunderstood what Jesus said: those who announced that their dead master had come back physically to life mistook a spiritual truth for an actual event.[38] But the true disciple may never have seen the earthly Jesus, having been born at the wrong time, as Paul said of himself.[39] Yet this physical disability may become a spiritual advantage: such persons, like Paul, may encounter Christ first on the level of inner experience.

How is Christ's presence experienced? The author of the *Gospel of Mary*, one of the few gnostic texts discovered before Nag Hammadi, interprets the resurrection appearances as visions received in dreams or in ecstatic trance. This gnostic gospel recalls traditions recorded in Mark and John, that Mary Magdalene was the first to see the risen Christ.[40] John says that Mary saw Jesus on the morning of his resurrection, and that he appeared to the other disciples only later, on the evening of the same day.[41] According to the *Gospel of Mary*, Mary Magdalene, seeing the Lord in a vision, asked him, "How does he who sees the vision see it? [Through] the soul, [or] through the spirit?"[42] He answered that the visionary perceives through the mind. The *Apocalypse of Peter*, discovered at Nag Hammadi, tells how

Peter, deep in trance, saw Christ, who explained that "I am the intellectual spirit, filled with radiant light."[43] Gnostic accounts often mention how the recipients respond to Christ's presence with intense emotions—terror, awe, distress, and joy.

Yet these gnostic writers do not dismiss visions as fantasies or hallucinations. They respect—even revere—such experiences, through which spiritual intuition discloses insight into the nature of reality. One gnostic teacher, whose *Treatise on Resurrection*, a letter to Rheginos, his student, was found at Nag Hammadi, says: "Do not suppose that resurrection is an apparition [*phantasia*; literally, "fantasy"]. It is not an apparition; rather it is something real. Instead," he continues, "one ought to maintain that the world is an apparition, rather than resurrection."[44] Like a Buddhist master, Rheginos' teacher, himself anonymous, goes on to explain that ordinary human existence is spiritual death. But the resurrection is the moment of enlightenment: "It is . . . the revealing of what truly exists . . . and a migration (*metabolē*—change, transition) into newness."[45] Whoever grasps this becomes spiritually alive. This means, he declares, that you can be "resurrected from the dead" right now: "Are you—the real you—mere corruption? . . . Why do you not examine your own self, and see that you have arisen?"[46] A third text from Nag Hammadi, the *Gospel of Philip*, expresses the same view, ridiculing ignorant Christians who take the resurrection literally. "Those who say they will die first and then rise are in error."[47] Instead they must "receive the resurrection while they live." The author says ironically that in one sense, then, of course "it is necessary to rise 'in this flesh,' since everything exists in it!"[48]

What interested these gnostics far more than past events attributed to the "historical Jesus" was the possibility of encountering the risen Christ in the present.[49] The *Gospel of Mary* illustrates the contrast between orthodox and gnostic viewpoints. The account recalls what Mark relates:

> Now when he rose early on the first day of the week, he appeared first to Mary Magdalene . . . She went and told

those who had been with him, as they mourned and wept. But when they heard that he was alive and had been seen by her, they would not believe it.[50]

As the *Gospel of Mary* opens, the disciples are mourning Jesus' death and terrified for their own lives. Then Mary Magdalene stands up to encourage them, recalling Christ's continual presence with them: "Do not weep, and do not grieve, and do not doubt; for his grace will be with you completely, and will protect you."[51] Peter invites Mary to "tell us the words of the Savior which you remember."[52] But to Peter's surprise, Mary does not tell anecdotes from the past; instead, she explains that she has just seen the Lord in a vision received through the mind, and she goes on to tell what he revealed to her. When Mary finishes,

> she fell silent, since it was to this point that the Savior had spoken with her. But Andrew answered and said to the brethren, "Say what you will about what she has said. I, at least, do not believe that the Savior has said this. For certainly these teachings are strange ideas!"[53]

Peter agrees with Andrew, ridiculing the idea that Mary actually saw the Lord in her vision. Then, the story continues,

> Mary wept and said to Peter, "My brother Peter, what do you think? Do you think that I thought this up myself in my heart? Do you think I am lying about the Savior?" Levi answered and said to Peter, "Peter, you have always been hot-tempered . . . If the Savior made her worthy, who are you to reject her?"[54]

Finally Mary, vindicated, joins the other apostles as they go out to preach. Peter, apparently representing the orthodox position, looks to past events, suspicious of those who "see the Lord" in visions: Mary, representing the gnostic, claims to experience his continuing presence.[55]

These gnostics recognized that their theory, like the orthodox one, bore political implications. It suggests that whoever "sees the Lord" through inner vision can claim that his or her own authority equals, or surpasses, that of the Twelve—and of their successors. Consider the political implications of the *Gospel of Mary*: Peter and Andrew, here representing the leaders of the orthodox group, accuse Mary—the gnostic—of pretending to have seen the Lord in order to justify the strange ideas, fictions, and lies she invents and attributes to divine inspiration. Mary lacks the proper credentials for leadership, from the orthodox viewpoint: she is not one of the "twelve." But as Mary stands up to Peter, so the gnostics who take her as their prototype challenge the authority of those priests and bishops who claim to be Peter's successors.

We know that gnostic teachers challenged the orthodox in precisely this way. While, according to them, the orthodox relied solely on the public, esoteric teaching which Christ and the apostles offered to "the many," gnostic Christians claimed to offer, in addition, their *secret* teaching, known only to the few.[56] The gnostic teacher and poet Valentinus (c. 140) points out that even during his lifetime, Jesus shared with his disciples certain mysteries, which he kept secret from outsiders.[57] According to the New Testament gospel of Mark, Jesus said to his disciples,

> . . . "To you has been given the secret of the kingdom of God, but for those outside everything is in parables; so that they may indeed see but not perceive, and may indeed hear but not understand; lest they should turn again, and be forgiven."[58]

Matthew, too, relates that when Jesus spoke in public, he spoke only in parables; when his disciples asked the reason, he replied, "To you it has been given to know the secrets [*mysteria*; literally, "mysteries"] of the kingdom of heaven, but to them it has not been given."[59] According to the gnostics, some of the disciples, following his instructions, kept secret Jesus' esoteric teaching: this they taught only in private, to certain persons who had proven themselves to be spiritually mature, and who therefore qualified for "initiation into *gnosis*"—that is, into secret knowledge.

Following the crucifixion, they allege that the risen Christ continued to reveal himself to certain disciples, opening to them, through visions, new insights into divine mysteries. Paul, referring to himself obliquely in the third person, says that he was "caught up to the third heaven—whether in the body or out of the body I do not know." There, in an ecstatic trance, he heard "things that cannot be told, which man may not utter."[60] Through his spiritual communication with Christ, Paul says he discovered "hidden mysteries" and "secret wisdom," which, he explains, he shares only with those Christians he considers "mature"[61] but not with everyone. Many contemporary Biblical scholars, themselves orthodox, have followed Rudolph Bultmann, who insists that Paul does not mean what he says in this passage.[62] They argue that Paul does *not* claim to have a secret tradition; such a claim would apparently make Paul sound too "gnostic." Recently Professor Robin Scroggs has taken the opposite view, pointing out that Paul clearly says that he *does* have secret wisdom.[63] Gnostic Christians in ancient times came to the same conclusion. Valentinus, the gnostic poet who traveled from Egypt to teach in Rome (c. 140), even claimed that he himself learned Paul's secret teaching from Theudas, one of Paul's own disciples.

Followers of Valentinus say that only their own gospels and revelations disclose those secret teachings. These writings tell countless stories about the risen Christ—the spiritual being whom Jesus represented—a figure who fascinated them far more than the merely human Jesus, the obscure rabbi from Nazareth. For this reason, gnostic writings often reverse the pattern of the New Testament gospels. Instead of telling the history of Jesus biographically, from birth to death, gnostic accounts begin where the others end—with stories of the spiritual Christ appearing to his disciples. The *Apocryphon of John*, for example, begins as John tells how he went out after the crucifixion in "great grief":

[15]

> Immediately . . . the [heavens were opened, and the whole] creation [which is] under heaven shone, and [the world] was shaken. [I was afraid, and I] saw in the light [a child] . . . while I looked he became like an old man. And he [changed his] form again, becoming like a servant . . . I saw . . . a[n image] with multiple forms in the light . . .[64]

As he marveled, the presence spoke:

> "John, Jo[h]n, why do you doubt, and why are you afraid? You are not unfamiliar with this form, are you? . . . Do not be afraid! I am the one who [is with you] always . . . [I have come to teach] you what is [and what was], and what will come to [be] . . ."[65]

The *Letter of Peter to Philip*, also discovered at Nag Hammadi, relates that after Jesus' death, the disciples were praying on the Mount of Olives when

> a great light appeared, so that the mountain shone from the sight of him who had appeared. And a voice called out to them saying "Listen . . . I am Jesus Christ, who is with you forever."[66]

Then, as the disciples ask him about the secrets of the universe, "a voice came out of the light" answering them. The *Wisdom of Jesus Christ* tells a similar story. Here again the disciples are gathered on a mountain after Jesus' death, when "then there appeared to them the Redeemer, not in his original form but in the invisible spirit. But his appearance was the appearance of a great angel of light." Responding to their amazement and terror, he smiles, and offers to teach them the "secrets [*mysteria*; literally, "mysteries"] of the holy plan" of the universe and its destiny.[67]

But the contrast with the orthodox view is striking.[68] Here Jesus does not appear in the ordinary human form the disciples recognize—and certainly not in *bodily* form. Either he appears as a luminous presence speaking out of the light, or he transforms himself into multiple forms. The *Gospel of Philip* takes up the same theme:

> Jesus took them all by stealth, for he did not reveal himself in the manner [in which] he was, but in the manner in which [they would] be able to see him. He revealed himself to [them all. He revealed himself] to the great as great . . . (and) to the small as small.[69]

To the immature disciple, Jesus appears as a child; to the mature, as an old man, symbol of wisdom. As the gnostic teacher Theodotus says, "each person recognizes the Lord in his own way, not all alike."[70]

Orthodox leaders, including Irenaeus, accused the gnostics of fraud. Such texts as those discovered at Nag Hammadi—the *Gospel of Thomas*, the *Gospel of Philip*, the *Letter of Peter to Philip*, and the *Apocryphon (Secret Book) of John*—proved, according to Irenaeus, that the heretics were trying to pass off as "apostolic" what they themselves had invented. He declares that the followers of the gnostic teacher Valentinus, being "utterly reckless,"

> put forth their own compositions, while boasting that they have more gospels than there really are . . . They really have no gospel which is not full of blasphemy. For what they have published . . . is totally unlike what has been handed down to us from the apostles.[71]

What proves the validity of the four gospels, Irenaeus says, is that they actually *were* written by Jesus' own disciples and their followers, who personally witnessed the events they described. Some contemporary Biblical scholars have challenged this view: few today believe that contemporaries of Jesus actually wrote the New Testament gospels. Although Irenaeus, defending their exclusive legitimacy, insisted that they were written by Jesus' own followers, we know virtually nothing about the persons who wrote the gospels we call Matthew, Mark, Luke, and John. We only know that these writings are attributed to apostles (Matthew and John) or followers of the apostles (Mark and Luke).

Gnostic authors, in the same way, attributed their secret writings to various disciples. Like those who wrote the New

Testament gospels, they may have received some of their material from early traditions. But in other cases, the accusation that the gnostics invented what they wrote contains some truth: certain gnostics openly acknowledged that they derived their *gnosis* from their own experience.

How, for example, could a Christian living in the second century write the *Secret Book of John?* We could imagine the author in the situation he attributes to John at the opening of the book: troubled by doubts, he begins to ponder the meaning of Jesus' mission and destiny. In the process of such internal questioning, answers may occur spontaneously to the mind; changing patterns of images may appear. The person who understands this process not in terms of modern psychology, as the activity of the imagination or unconscious, but in religious terms, could experience these as forms of spiritual communication with Christ. Seeing his own communion with Christ as a continuation of what the disciples enjoyed, the author, when he casts the "dialogue" into literary form, could well give to them the role of the questioners. Few among his contemporaries—except the orthodox, whom he considers "literal-minded"—would accuse him of forgery; rather, the titles of these works indicate that they were written "in the spirit" of John, Mary Magdalene, Philip, or Peter.

Attributing a writing to a specific apostle may also bear a symbolic meaning. The title of the *Gospel of Mary* suggests that its revelation came from a direct, intimate communication with the Savior. The hint of an erotic relationship between him and Mary Magdalene may indicate claims to mystical communion; throughout history, mystics of many traditions have chosen sexual metaphors to describe their experiences. The titles of the *Gospel of Thomas* and the *Book of Thomas the Contender* (attributed to Jesus' "twin brother") may suggest that "you, the reader, are Jesus' twin brother." Whoever comes to understand these books discovers, like Thomas, that Jesus is his "twin," his spiritual "other self." Jesus' words to Thomas, then, are addressed to the reader:

[18]

"Since it has been said that you are my twin and true companion, examine yourself so that you may understand who you are . . . I am the knowledge of the truth. So while you accompany me, although you do not understand (it), you already have come to know, and you will be called 'the one who knows himself.' For whoever has not known himself has known nothing, but whoever has known himself has simultaneously achieved knowledge about the depth of all things."[72]

Like circles of artists today, gnostics considered original creative invention to be the mark of anyone who becomes spiritually alive. Each one, like students of a painter or writer, expected to express his own perceptions by revising and transforming what he was taught. Whoever merely repeated his teacher's words was considered immature. Bishop Irenaeus complains that

> every one of them generates something new every day, according to his ability; for no one is considered initiated [or: "mature"] among them unless he develops some enormous fictions![73]

He charges that "they boast that they are the discoverers and inventors of this kind of imaginary fiction," and accuses them of creating new forms of mythological poetry. No doubt he is right: first- and second-century gnostic literature includes some remarkable poems, like the "Round Dance of the Cross"[74] and the "Thunder, Perfect Mind." Most offensive, from his point of view, is that they admit that nothing supports their writings except their own intuition. When challenged, "they either mention mere human feelings, or else refer to the harmony that can be seen in creation":[75]

> They are to be blamed for . . . describing human feelings, and passions, and mental tendencies . . . and ascribing the things that happen to human beings, and *whatever they recognize themselves as experiencing*, to the divine Word.[76]

[19]

On this basis, like artists, they express their own insight—their own *gnosis*—by creating new myths, poems, rituals, "dialogues" with Christ, revelations, and accounts of their visions.

Like Baptists, Quakers, and many others, the gnostic is convinced that whoever receives the spirit communicates directly with the divine. One of Valentinus' students, the gnostic teacher Heracleon (c. 160), says that "at first, people believe because of the testimony of others . . ." but then "they come to believe from the truth itself."[77] So his own teacher, Valentinus, claimed to have first learned Paul's secret teaching; then he experienced a vision which became the source of his own *gnosis*:

> He saw a newborn infant, and when he asked who he might be, the child answered, "I am the Logos."[78]

Marcus, another student of Valentinus' (c. 150), who went on to become a teacher himself, tells how he came to his own firsthand knowledge of the truth. He says that a vision

> descended upon him . . . in the form of a woman . . . and expounded to him alone its own nature, and the origin of things, which it had never revealed to anyone, divine or human.[79]

The presence then said to him,

> "I wish to show you Truth herself; for I have brought her down from above, so that you may see her without a veil, and understand her beauty."[80]

And that, Marcus adds, is how "the naked Truth" came to him in a woman's form, disclosing her secrets to him. Marcus expects, in turn, that everyone whom he initiates into *gnosis* will also receive such experiences. In the initiation ritual, after invoking the spirit, he commands the candidate to speak in prophecy,[81] to demonstrate that the person has received direct contact with the divine.

What differentiates these gnostics from those who, throughout the history of Christianity, have claimed to receive special visions and revelations, and who have expressed these in art, poetry, and mystical literature? Christians who stand in orthodox tradition, Catholics and Protestants, expect that the revelations they receive will confirm (in principle, at least) apostolic tradition: this, they agree, sets the boundaries of Christian faith. The apostles' original teaching remains the criterion; whatever deviates is heresy. Bishop Irenaeus declares that the apostles,

> like a rich man (depositing money) in a bank, placed in the church fully everything that belongs to truth: so that everyone, whoever will, can draw from her the water of life.[82]

The orthodox Christian believes "the one and only truth from the apostles, which is handed down by the church." And he accepts no gospels but the four in the New Testament which serve as the canon (literally, "guideline") to measure all future doctrine and practice.

But the gnostic Christians, whom Irenaeus opposed, assumed that they had gone far beyond the apostles' original teaching. Just as many people today assume that the most recent experiments in science or psychology will surpass earlier ones, so the gnostics anticipated that the present and future would yield a continual increase in knowledge. Irenaeus takes this as proof of their arrogance:

> They consider themselves "mature," so that no one can be compared with them in the greatness of their *gnosis*, not even if you mention Peter or Paul or any of the other apostles. . . . They imagine that they themselves have discovered more than the apostles, and that the apostles preached the gospel still under the influence of Jewish opinions, but that they themselves are wiser and more intelligent than the apostles.[83]

And those who consider themselves "wiser than the apostles" also consider themselves "wiser than the priests."[84] For what the gnostics say about the apostles—and, in particular, about the Twelve—expresses their attitude toward the priests and bishops, who claim to stand in the orthodox apostolic succession.

But despite their emphasis on free creativity, some gnostic

teachers—rather inconsistently—claim to have their own, secret sources of "apostolic tradition." Thereby they claim access to different lines of apostolic sucession from that commonly accepted in the churches. The gnostic teacher Ptolemy explains to Flora, a woman he sees as a potential initiate, that "we too have received" apostolic tradition from a sucession of teachers— one that, he says, offers an esoteric supplement to the canonical collection of Jesus' words.[85]

Gnostic authors often attribute their own traditions to persons who stand *outside* the circle of the Twelve—Paul, Mary Magdalene, and James. Some insist that the Twelve—including Peter—had not received *gnosis* when they first witnessed to Christ's resurrection. Another group of gnostics, called Sethians because they identified themselves as sons of Seth, the third child of Adam and Eve, say that the disciples, deluded by "a very great error," imagined that Christ had risen from the dead in bodily form. But the risen Christ appeared to "a few of these disciples, who he recognized were capable of understanding such great mysteries,"[86] and taught them to understand his resurrection in spiritual, not physical, terms. Furthermore, as we have seen, the *Gospel of Mary* depicts Mary Magdalene (never recognized as an apostle by the orthodox) as the one favored with visions and insight that far surpass Peter's. The *Dialogue of the Savior* praises her not only as a visionary, but as the apostle who excels all the rest. She is the "woman who knew the All."[87] Valentinus claims that his apostolic tradition comes from Paul—another outsider to the Twelve, but one of the greatest authorities of the orthodox, and, after Luke, the author most extensively represented in the New Testament.

Other gnostics explain that certain members of the Twelve later received special visions and revelations, and so attained enlightenment. The *Apocalypse of Peter* describes how Peter, deep in trance, experiences the presence of Christ, who opens his eyes to spiritual insight:

> [The Savior] said to me . . . , ". . . put your hands upon (your) eyes . . . and say what you see!" But when I

had done it, I did not see anything. I said, "No one sees (this way)." Again he told me, "Do it again." And there came into me fear with joy, for I saw a new light, greater than the light of day. Then it came down upon the Savior. And I told him about the things which I saw.[88]

The *Secret Book of James* tells how "the twelve disciples were all sitting together and recalling what the Savior had said to each one of them, whether in secret or openly, and [setting it in order] in books."[89] But when Christ appeared, he chose Peter and James, and drew them apart from the rest to tell them what the others were not to know. Either version of this theory bears the same implication: it asserts the superiority of gnostic forms of secret tradition—and hence, of gnostic teachers—over that of the priests and bishops, who can offer only "common" tradition. Further, because earlier traditions, from this point of view, are at best incomplete, and at worst simply false, gnostic Christians continually drew upon their own spiritual experience—their own *gnosis*—to revise and transform them.

But what gnostics celebrated as proof of spiritual maturity, the orthodox denounced as "deviation" from apostolic tradition. Tertullian finds it outrageous that

> every one of them, just as it suits his own temperament, modifies the traditions he has received, just as the one who handed them down modified them, when he shaped them according to his own will.[90]

That they "disagree on specific matters, even from their own founders" meant to Tertullian that they were "unfaithful" to apostolic tradition. Diversity of teaching was the very mark of heresy:

> On what grounds are heretics strangers and enemies to the apostles, if it is not from the difference of their teaching, which each individual of his own mere will has either advanced or received?[91]

Doctrinal conformity defined the orthodox faith. Bishop Irenaeus declares that the catholic church believes these points of doctrine just as if she had only one soul, and one and the same heart, and she proclaims them and teaches them in perfect harmony. . . . For although the languages of the world are different, still the meaning of the tradition is one and the same. For the churches which have been planted in Germany do not believe or hand down anything different, nor do those in Spain, nor those in Gaul, nor those in the east, nor those in Egypt, nor those in Africa, nor those which have been established in the central regions of the world.[92]

What would happen if arguments did arise among such scattered churches? Who should decide which traditions would take priority? Irenaeus considers the question:

> But how is it? Suppose a dispute concerning some important question arises among us; should we not have recourse to the most ancient churches, with which the apostles held continual intercourse, and learn from them what is clear and certain in regard to the present question?[93]

Irenaeus prescribes terminating any disagreement

> by indicating that tradition, derived-from the apostles, of the very great, the very ancient, and universally known church founded and organized at Rome by the two most glorious apostles, Peter and Paul . . . and by indicating the faith . . . which came down to our time by means of the succession of the bishops. For it is necessary that every church should agree with this church, on account of its preeminent authority.[94]

Since no one of later generations can have access to Christ as the apostles did, during his lifetime and at his resurrection, every believer must look to the church at Rome, which they founded, and to the bishops for authority.

Some gnostic Christians counterattacked. The *Apocalypse of Peter*, probably among the latest writings discovered at Nag Hammadi (c. 200–300), tells how dismayed Peter was to hear that many believers "will fall into an erroneous name" and "will be ruled heretically."[95] The risen Christ explains to Peter that those who "name themselves bishop, and also deacon, as if they had received their authority from God," are, in reality, "waterless canals."[96] Although they "do not understand mystery," they "boast that the mystery of truth belongs to them alone."[97] The author accuses them of having misinterpreted the apostles' teaching, and thus having set up an "imitation church" in place of the true Christian "brotherhood."[98] Other gnostics, including the followers of Valentinus, did not challenge the bishop's right to teach the common apostolic tradition. Nor did they oppose, in principle, the leadership of priests and bishops. But for them the church's teaching, and the church officials, could never hold the ultimate authority which orthodox Christians accorded them.[99] All who had received *gnosis*, they say, had gone beyond the church's teaching and had transcended the authority of its hierarchy.

The controversy over resurrection, then, proved critical in shaping the Christian movement into an institutional religion. All Christians agreed in principle that only Christ himself—or God—can be the ultimate source of spiritual authority. But the immediate question, of course, was the practical one: Who, in the present, administers that authority?

Valentinus and his followers answered: Whoever comes into direct, personal contact with the "living One." They argued that only one's own experience offers the ultimate criterion of truth, taking precedence over all secondhand testimony and all tradition—even gnostic tradition! They celebrated every form of creative invention as evidence that a person has become spiritually alive. On this theory, the structure of authority can never be fixed into an institutional framework: it must remain spontaneous, charismatic, and open.

Those who rejected this theory argued that all future generations of Christians must trust the apostles' testimony—even more than their own experience. For, as Tertullian admitted, whoever judges in terms of ordinary historical experience would find the claim that a man physically returned from the grave to be incredible. What can never be proven or verified in the present, Tertullian says, "must be believed, because it is absurd." Since the death of the apostles, believers must accept the word of the priests and bishops, who have claimed, from the second century, to be their only legitimate heirs.

Recognizing the political implications of the doctrine of resurrection does not account for its extraordinary impact on the religious experience of Christians. Whoever doubts that impact has only to recall any of the paintings it evoked from artists as diverse as Della Francesca, Michelangelo, Rembrandt, and Dali, or the music written on the theme by composers from ancient times through Bach, Mozart, Handel, and Mahler.

The conviction that a man who died came back to life is, of course, a paradox. But that paradox may contain the secret of its powerful appeal, for while it contradicts our own historical experience, it speaks the language of human emotions. It addresses itself to that which may be our deepest fear, and expresses our longing to overcome death.

The contemporary theologian Jürgen Moltmann suggests that the orthodox view of resurrection also expressed, in symbolic language, the conviction that human life is inseparable from bodily experience: even if a man comes back to life from the dead, he must come back *physically*.[100] Irenaeus and Tertullian both emphasize that the anticipation of bodily resurrection requires believers to take seriously the ethical implications of their own actions. Certainly it is true that gnostics who ridiculed the idea of bodily resurrection frequently devalued the body, and considered its actions (sexual acts, for example) unimportant to the "spiritual" person. According to the *Gospel of Thomas*, for example, Jesus says,

> "If spirit came into being because of the body, it is a wonder of wonders. Indeed, I am amazed at how this great wealth [the spirit] has made its home in this poverty [the body]."[101]

For the gnostics stood close to the Greek philosophic tradition (and, for that matter, to Hindu and Buddhist tradition) that regards the human spirit as residing "in" a body—as if the actual person were some sort of disembodied being who uses the body as an instrument but does not identify with it. Those who agree with Moltmann may find, then, that the orthodox doctrine of resurrection, far from negating bodily experience, affirmed it as the central fact of human life.

But in terms of the social order, as we have seen, the orthodox teaching on resurrection had a different effect: it legitimized a hierarchy of persons through whose authority all others must approach God. Gnostic teaching, as Irenaeus and Tertullian realized, was potentially subversive of this order: it claimed to offer to every initiate direct access to God of which the priests and bishops themselves might be ignorant.[102]

CHAPTER
II

"One God, One Bishop": The Politics of Monotheism

THE CHRISTIAN CREED begins with the words "I believe in one God, Father Almighty, Maker of heaven and earth." Some scholars suggest that this credal statement was originally formulated to exclude followers of the heretic Marcion (c. 140) from orthodox churches. A Christian from Asia Minor, Marcion was struck by what he saw as the contrast between the creator-God of the Old Testament, who demands justice and punishes every violation of his law, and the Father whom Jesus proclaims—the New Testament God of forgiveness and love. Why, he asked, would a God who is "almighty"—all-powerful —create a world that includes suffering, pain, disease—even mosquitoes and scorpions? Marcion concluded that these must be two different Gods. The majority of Christians early condemned this view as dualistic, and identified themselves as orthodox by confessing one God, who is both "Father Almighty" and "Maker of heaven and earth."

When advocates of orthodoxy confronted another challenge —the gnostics—they often attacked them as "Marcionites" and "dualists." Irenaeus states as his major complaint against the gnostics that they, like the Marcionites, say that "there is another God besides the creator." Some of the recently discovered texts confirm his account. According to the *Hypostasis of the Archons*, the creator's vain claim[1] to hold an exclusive monopoly on divine power shows that he

> is blind . . . [because of his] power and his ignorance [and his] arrogance he said . . . , "It is I who am God; there is none [other apart from me]." When he said this, he sinned against [the Entirety]. And a voice came forth from above the realm of absolute power, saying, "You are mistaken, Samael," which means, "god of the blind."[2]

Another text discovered in the same codex at Nag Hammadi, *On the Origin of the World*, tells a variant of the same story:

> . . . he boasted continually, saying to (the angels) . . . "I am God, and no other one exists except me." But when he said these things, he sinned against all of the immortal ones . . . when Faith saw the impiety of the chief ruler, she was angry. . . . she said, "You err, Samael (i.e., "blind god"). An enlightened, immortal humanity [*anthropos*] exists before you!"[3]

A third text bound into the same volume, the *Secret Book of John*, relates how

> in his madness . . . he said, "I am God, and there is no other God beside me," for he is ignorant of . . . the place from which he had come. . . . And when he saw the creation which surrounds him and the multitudes of angels around him which had come forth from him, he said to them, "I am a jealous God, and there is no other God beside me." But by announcing this he indicated to the angels that another God does exist; for if there were no other one, of whom would he be jealous?[4]

When these same sources tell the story of the Garden of Eden, they characterize this God as the jealous master, whose tyranny the serpent (often, in ancient times, a symbol of divine wisdom) taught Adam and Eve to resist:

> . . . God gave [a command] to Adam, "From every [tree] you may eat, [but] from the tree which is in the midst of Paradise do not eat, for on the day that you eat from it you will surely die." But the serpent was wiser than all the animals that were in Paradise, and he persuaded Eve, saying, "On the day when you eat from the tree which is in the midst of Paradise, the eyes of your mind will be opened." And Eve obeyed . . . she ate; she also gave to her husband.[5]

Observing that the serpent's promise came true—their eyes were opened—but that God's threat of immediate death did not, the gnostic author goes on to quote God's words from Genesis 3:22, adding editorial comment:

> . . . "Behold, Adam has become like one of us, knowing evil and good." Then he said, "Let us cast him out of Paradise, lest he take from the tree of life, and live forever." But of what sort is this God? First [he] envied Adam that he should eat from the tree of knowledge. . . . Surely he has shown himself to be a malicious envier.[6]

As the American scholar Birger Pearson points out, the author uses an Aramaic pun to equate the serpent with the Instructor ("serpent," *hewyā*; "to instruct," *ḥawā*).[7] Other gnostic accounts add a four-way pun that includes Eve (Ḥawāh): instead of tempting Adam, she gives life to him and instructs him:

> After the day of rest, Sophia [literally, "wisdom"] sent Zoe [literally, "life"], her daughter, who is called Eve, as an instructor to raise up Adam . . . When Eve saw Adam cast down, she pitied him, and she said, "Adam, live! Rise up upon the earth!" Immediately her word became a deed. For when Adam rose up, immediately he opened his eyes. When he saw her, he said, "You will be called 'the mother of the living,' because you are the one who gave me life."[8]

The *Hypostasis of the Archons* describes Eve as the spiritual principle in humanity who raises Adam from his merely material condition:

> And the spirit-endowed Woman came to [Adam] and spoke with him, saying, "Arise, Adam." And when he saw her, he said, "It is you who have given me life; you shall be called "Mother of the living"—for it is she who is my mother. It is she who is the Physician, and the Woman, and She Who Has Given Birth." . . . Then the Female Spiritual Principle came in the Snake, the Instructor, and it taught them, saying, ". . . you shall not die; for it was out of jealousy that he said this to you. Rather, your eyes shall open, and you shall become like gods, recognizing evil and good." . . . And the arrogant Ruler cursed the Woman . . . [and] . . . the Snake.[9]

Some scholars today consider gnosticism synonymous with metaphysical dualism—or even with pluralities of gods. Irenaeus denounced as blasphemy such caricatures of the conviction, fundamental to the Hebrew Scriptures, that "the Lord your God is one God." But Clement of Alexandria, Irenaeus' contemporary, tells us that there was a "monadic *gnosis*"; and the discoveries at Nag Hammadi also disclose that Valentinian gnosticism—the most influential and sophisticated form of gnostic teaching, and by far the most threatening to the church—differs essentially from dualism. The theme of the oneness of God dominates the opening section of the *Tripartite Tractate*, a Valentinian treatise from Nag Hammadi which describes the origin of all being. The author describes God as

> a sole Lord and God . . . For he is unbegotten . . . In the proper sense, then, the only Father and God is the one whom no one else begot. As for the universe (*cosmos*), he is the one who begot and created it.[10]

A Valentinian Exposition speaks of God who is

> [Root] of the All, the [Ineffable One who] dwells in the Monad. [He dwells alone] in silence . . . since, after all, [he was] a Monad, and no one was before him . . .[11]

According to a third Valentinian text, the *Interpretation of Knowledge*, the Savior taught that "Your Father, who is in heaven, is one."[12]

Irenaeus himself tells us that the creed which effectively screened out Marcionites from the church proved useless against the Valentinians. In common with other Christians, they recited the orthodox creed. But Irenaeus explains that although they did "verbally confess one God," they did so with private mental reservations, "saying one thing, and thinking another."[13] While the Marcionites openly blasphemed the creator, the Valentinians, he insists, did so covertly:

> Such persons are, to outward appearances, sheep, for they seem to be like us, from what they say in public, repeating the same words [of confession] that we do; but inwardly they are wolves.[14]

What distressed Irenaeus most was that the majority of Christians did not recognize the followers of Valentinus as heretics. Most could not tell the difference between Valentinian and orthodox teaching; after all, he says, most people cannot differentiate between cut glass and emeralds either! But, he declares, "although their language is similar to ours," their views "not only are very different, but at all points full of blasphemies."[15] The apparent similarity with orthodox teaching only made this heresy more dangerous—like poison disguised as milk. So he wrote the five volumes of his massive *Refutation and Overthrow of Falsely So-called Gnosis* to teach the unwary to discriminate between the truth, which saves believers, and gnostic teaching, which destroys them in "an abyss of madness and blasphemy."[16]

For while the Valentinians publicly confessed faith in one God,[17] in their own private meetings they insisted on discriminating between the popular image of God—as master, king, lord, creator, and judge—and what that image represented—God understood as the ultimate source of all being.[18] Valentinus calls that source "the depth";[19] his followers describe it as an invisible, incomprehensible primal principle.[20] But most Christians, they say, mistake mere images of God for that reality.[21] They point out that the Scriptures sometimes depict God as a mere crafts-man, or as an avenging judge, as a king who rules in heaven, or even as a jealous master. But these images, they say, cannot compare with Jesus' teaching that "God is spirit" or the "Father of Truth."[22] Another Valentinian, the author of the *Gospel of Philip*, points out that names can be

> very deceptive, for they divert our thoughts from what is accurate to what is inaccurate. Thus one who hears the word "God" does not perceive what is accurate, but perceives what is inaccurate. So also with "the Father," and "the Son," and "the Holy Spirit," and "life," and "light," and "resurrec-tion," and "the Church," and all the rest—people do not perceive what is accurate, but they perceive what is in-accurate . . .[23]

The Protestant theologian Paul Tillich recently drew a similar distinction between the God we imagine when we hear the term, and the "God beyond God," that is, the "ground of being" that underlies all our concepts and images.

What made their position heretical? Why did Irenaeus find such a modification of monotheism so crucial—in fact, so utterly reprehensible—that he urged his fellow believers to expel the followers of Valentinus from the churches as heretics? He admitted that this question puzzled the gnostics themselves:

> They ask, when they confess the same things and par-ticipate in the same worship . . . how is it that we, for no reason, remain aloof from them; and how is it that when they confess the same things, and hold the same doctrines, *we call them heretics!*[24]

I suggest that here again we cannot fully answer this question as long as we consider this debate exclusively in terms of religious and philosophical arguments. But when we investigate how the doctrine of God actually functions in gnostic and orthodox writings, we can see how this religious question also involves social and political issues. Specifically, by the latter part of the second century, when the orthodox insisted upon "one God," they simultaneously validated the system of governance in which the church is ruled by "one bishop." Gnostic modification of monotheism was taken—and perhaps intended—as an attack upon that system. For when gnostic and orthodox Christians discussed the nature of God, they were at the same time debating the issue of *spiritual authority*.

This issue dominates one of the earliest writings we have from the church at Rome—a letter attributed to Clement, called Bishop of Rome (c. 90–100). As spokesman for the Roman church, Clement wrote to the Christian community in Corinth at a time of crisis: certain leaders of the Corinthian church had been divested of power. Clement says that "a few rash and self-willed people" drove them out of office: "those of no reputation [rose up] against those with reputation, the fools against the wise, the young against the old."[25] Using political language, he calls this "a rebellion"[26] and insists that the deposed leaders be restored to their authority: he warns that they must be feared, respected, and obeyed.

On what grounds? Clement argues that God, the God of Israel, alone rules all things:[27] he is the lord and master whom all must obey; he is the judge who lays down the law, punishing rebels and rewarding the obedient. But how is God's rule actually administered? Here Clement's theology becomes practical: God, he says, delegates his "authority of reign" to "rulers and leaders on earth."[28] Who are these designated rulers? Clement answers that they are bishops, priests, and deacons. Whoever refuses to "bow the neck"[29] and obey the church leaders is guilty of insubordination against the divine master himself. Carried away with his argument, Clement warns that whoever disobeys the divinely ordained authorities "receives the death penalty!"[30]

This letter marks a dramatic moment in the history of Christianity. For the first time, we find here an argument for dividing the Christian community between "the clergy" and "the laity." The church is to be organized in terms of a strict order of superiors and subordinates. Even within the clergy, Clement insists on ranking each member, whether bishop, priest, or deacon, "in his own order":[31] each must observe "the rules and commandments" of his position at all times.

Many historians are puzzled by this letter.[32] What, they ask, was the basis for the dispute in Corinth? What *religious* issues were at stake? The letter does not tell us that directly. But this does not mean that the author ignores such issues. I suggest that he makes his own point—his religious point—entirely clear: he intended to establish the Corinthian church on the model of the divine authority. As God reigns in heaven as master, lord, commander, judge, and king, so on earth he delegates his rule to members of the church hierarchy, who serve as generals who command an army of subordinates; kings who rule over "the people"; judges who preside in God's place.

Clement may simply be stating what Roman Christians took for granted[33]—and what Christians outside of Rome, in the early second century, were coming to accept. The chief advocates of this theory, not surprisingly, were the bishops themselves. Only a generation later, another bishop, Ignatius of Antioch in Syria, more than a thousand miles from Rome, passionately defended the same principle. But Ignatius went further than Clement. He defended the three ranks—bishop, priests, and deacons—as a hierarchical order that mirrors the divine hierarchy in heaven. As there is only one God in heaven, Ignatius declares, so there can be only one bishop in the church. "One God, one bishop"— this became the orthodox slogan. Ignatius warns "the laity" to revere, honor, and obey the bishop "as if he were God." For the bishop, standing at the pinnacle of the church hierarchy, presides "in the place of God."[34] Who, then, stands below God? The divine council, Ignatius replies. And as God rules over that council in heaven, so the bishop on earth rules over a council of priests. The heavenly divine council, in turn, stands above the apostles; so, on earth, the priests rule over the deacons—and all three of these rule over "the laity."[35]

Was Ignatius merely attempting to aggrandize his own

position? A cynical observer might suspect him of masking power politics with religious rhetoric. But the distinction between religion and politics, so familiar to us in the twentieth century, was utterly alien to Ignatius' self-understanding. For him, as for his contemporaries, pagan and Christian alike, religious convictions necessarily involved political relationships —and vice versa. Ironically, Ignatius himself shared this view with the Roman officials who condemned him to death, judging his religious convictions as evidence for treason against Rome. For Ignatius, as for Roman pagans, politics and religion formed an inseparable unity. He believed that God became accessible to humanity *through the church*—and specifically, through the bishops, priests, and deacons who administer it: "without these, there is nothing which can be called a church!"[36] For the sake of their eternal salvation he urged people to submit themselves to the bishop and priests. Although Ignatius and Clement depicted the structure of the clergy in different ways,[37] both bishops agreed that this human order mirrors the divine authority in heaven. Their religious views, certainly, bore political implications; yet, at the same time, the practice they urged was based on their beliefs about God.

What would happen if someone challenged their doctrine of God—as the one who stands at the pinnacle of the divine hierarchy and legitimizes the whole structure? We do not have to guess: we can see what happened when Valentinus went from Egypt to Rome (c. 140). Even his enemies spoke of him as a brilliant and eloquent man:[38] his admirers revered him as a poet and spiritual master. One tradition attributes to him the poetic, evocative *Gospel of Truth* that was discovered at Nag Hammadi. Valentinus claims that besides receiving the Christian tradition that all believers hold in common, he has received from Theudas, a disciple of Paul's, initiation into a secret doctrine of God.[39] Paul himself taught this secret wisdom, he says, not to everyone, and not publicly, but only to a select few whom he considered to be spiritually mature.[40] Valentinus offers, in turn, to initiate "those who are mature"[41] into his wisdom, since not everyone is able to comprehend it.

What this secret tradition reveals is that the one whom most Christians naïvely worship as creator, God, and Father is, in reality, only the image of the true God. According to Valentinus, what Clement and Ignatius mistakenly ascribe to God actually applies only to the *creator*.[42] Valentinus, following Plato, uses the Greek term for "creator" (*demiurgos*),[43] suggesting that he is a lesser divine being who serves as the instrument of the higher powers.[44] It is not God, he explains, but the demiurge who reigns as king and lord,[45] who acts as a military commander,[46] who gives the law and judges those who violate it[47]—in short, he is the "God of Israel."

Through the initiation Valentinus offers, the candidate learns to reject the creator's authority and all his demands as foolishness. What gnostics know is that the creator makes false claims to power ("I am God, and there is no other")[48] that derive from his own ignorance. Achieving *gnosis* involves coming to recognize the true source of divine power—namely, "the depth" of all being. Whoever has come to know that source simultaneously comes to know himself and discovers his spiritual origin: he has come to know his true Father and Mother.

Whoever comes to this *gnosis*—this insight—is ready to receive the secret sacrament called the redemption (*apolytrosis*; literally, "release").[49] Before gaining *gnosis*, the candidate worshiped the demiurge, mistaking him for the true God: now, through the sacrament of redemption, the candidate indicates that he has been released from the demiurge's power. In this ritual he addresses the demiurge, declaring his independence, serving notice that he no longer belongs to the demiurge's sphere of authority and judgment,[50] but to what transcends it:

I am a son from the Father—the Father who is pre-existent. . . . I derive being from Him who is preexistent, and I come again to my own place whence I came forth.[51]

What are the practical—even political—implications of this religious theory? Consider how Valentinus or one of his initiates might respond to Clement's claim that the bishop rules over the community "as God rules in heaven"—as master, king, judge, and lord. Would not an initiate be likely to reply to such a bishop: "You claim to represent God, but, in reality, you represent only the demiurge, whom you blindly serve and obey. I, however, have passed beyond the sphere of his authority—and so, for that matter, beyond yours!"

Irenaeus, as bishop, recognized the danger to clerical authority. The redemption ritual, which dramatically changed the initiate's relation to the demiurge, changed simultaneously his relationship to the bishop. Before, the believer was taught to submit to the bishop "as to God himself," since, he was told, the bishop rules, commands, and judges "in God's place." But now he sees that such restrictions apply only to naïve believers who still fear and serve the demiurge.[52] *Gnosis* offers nothing less than a theological justification for refusing to obey the bishops and priests! The initiate now sees them as the "rulers and powers" who rule on earth in the demiurge's name. The gnostic admits that the bishop, like the demiurge, exercises legitimate authority over most Christians—those who are uninitiated.[53] But the bishop's demands, warnings, and threats, like those of the demiurge himself, can no longer touch the one who has been "redeemed." Irenaeus explains the effect of this ritual:

> They maintain that they have attained to a height beyond every power, and that therefore they are free in every respect to act as they please, having no one to fear in anything. For they claim that because of the *redemption* . . . they cannot be apprehended, or even perceived, by the judge.[54]

The candidate receives from his initiation into *gnosis* an entirely new relation to spiritual authority. Now he knows that the clerical hierarchy derives its authority from the demiurge—not from the Father. When a bishop like Clement commands the believer to "fear God" or to "confess that you have a Lord," or when Irenaeus warns that "God will judge" the sinner, the gnostic may hear all of these as their attempt to reassert the false claims of the demiurge's power, and of his earthly representatives, over the believer. In the demiurge's foolish assertion that "I am God, and there is no other," the gnostic could hear the bishop's claim to exercise exclusive power over the community. In his warning, "I am a jealous God," the gnostic might recognize the bishop's jealousy for those who are beyond his authority. Bishop Irenaeus, in turn, satirizes their tantalizing and seductive style:

> If anyone yields himself to them like a little sheep, and follows out their practice and their *redemption*, such a person becomes so puffed up that . . . he walks with a strutting gait and a supercilious countenance, possessing all the pompous air of a cock![55]

Tertullian traces such arrogance to the example of their teacher Valentinus, who, he says, refused to submit himself to the superior authority of the bishop of Rome. For what reason? Tertullian says that Valentinus wanted to become bishop himself. But when another man was chosen instead, he was filled with envy and frustrated ambition, and cut himself off from the church to found a rival group of his own.[56]

Few historians believe Tertullian's story. In the first place, it follows a typical polemic against heresy which maintains that envy and ambition lead heretics to deviate from the true faith. Second, some twenty years after this alleged incident, followers of Valentinus considered themselves to be fully members of the church, and indignantly resisted orthodox attempts to expel them.[57] This suggests that the orthodox, rather than those they called heretics, initiated the break.

Yet Tertullian's story, even—perhaps especially—if untrue, illustrates what many Christians saw as one of the dangers of heresy: it encourages insubordination to clerical authority. And, apparently, the orthodox were right. Bishop Irenaeus tells us that followers of Valentinus "assemble in unauthorized meetings"[58]—

that is, in meetings that he himself, as bishop, has not authorized. At these meetings they attempted to raise doubts in the minds of their hearers: Does the church's teaching really satisfy them, or not?[59] Have the sacraments which the church dispenses—baptism and the eucharist—given them a complete initiation into Christian faith, or only the first step?[60] Members of the inner circle suggested that what the bishop and priests taught publicly were only *elementary* doctrines. They themselves claimed to offer more—the secret mysteries, the higher teachings.

This controversy occurred at the very time when earlier, diversified forms of church leadership were giving way to a unified hierarchy of church office.[61] For the first time, certain Christian communities were organizing into a strict order of subordinate "ranks" of bishops, priests, deacons, laity. In many churches the bishop was emerging, for the first time, as a "monarch" (literally, "sole ruler"). Increasingly, he claimed the power to act as disciplinarian and judge over those he called "the laity." Could certain gnostic movements represent resistance to this process? Could gnostics stand among the critics who opposed the development of church hierarchy? Evidence from Nag Hammadi suggests that they did. We have noted before how the author of the *Apocalypse of Peter* ridicules the claims of church officials:

> Others . . . outside our number . . . call themselves bishops and also deacons, as if they had received their authority from God. . . . Those people are waterless canals.[62]

The *Tripartite Tractate*, written by a follower of Valentinus, contrasts those who are gnostics, "children of the Father," with those who are uninitiates, offspring of the demiurge.[63] The Father's children, he says, join together as equals, enjoying mutual love, spontaneously helping one another. But the demiurge's offspring—the ordinary Christians—"wanted to command one another, outrivalling one another in their empty ambition"; they are inflated with "lust for power," "each one imagining that he is superior to the others."[64]

If gnostic Christians criticized the development of church hierarchy, how could they themselves form a social organization? If they rejected the principle of rank, insisting that all are equal, how could they even hold a meeting? Irenaeus tells us about the practice of one group that he knows from his own congregation in Lyons—the group led by Marcus, a disciple of Valentinus'.[65] Every member of the group had been initiated: this meant that every one had been "released" from the demiurge's power. For this reason, they dared to meet without the authority of the bishop, whom they regarded as the demiurge's spokesman— Irenaeus himself! Second, every initiate was assumed to have received, through the initiation ritual, the charismatic gift of direct inspiration through the Holy Spirit.[66]

How did members of this circle of "pneumatics" (literally, "those who are spiritual") conduct their meetings? Irenaeus tells us that when they met, all the members first participated in drawing lots.[67] Whoever received a certain lot apparently was designated to take the role of *priest*; another was to offer the sacrament, as *bishop*; another would read the Scriptures for worship, and others would address the group as a *prophet*, offering extemporaneous spiritual instruction. The next time the group met, they would throw lots again so that the persons taking each role changed continually.

This practice effectively created a very different structure of authority. At a time when the orthodox Christians increasingly discriminated between clergy and laity, this group of gnostic Christians demonstrated that, among themselves, they refused to acknowledge such distinctions. Instead of ranking their members into superior and inferior "orders" within a hierarchy, they followed the principle of strict equality. All initiates, men and women alike, participated equally in the drawing; anyone might be selected to serve as *priest, bishop,* or *prophet*. Furthermore, because they cast lots at each meeting, even the distinctions established by lot could never become permanent "ranks." Finally—most important—they intended, through this practice, to remove the element of human choice. A twentieth-century observer might assume that the gnostics left these matters to random chance, but the gnostics saw it differently. They believed that since God directs everything in the universe, the way the lots fell expressed his choice.

Such practices prompted Tertullian to attack "the behavior of the heretics":

> How frivolous, how worldly, how merely *human* it is, without seriousness, without authority, without discipline, as fits their faith! To begin with, it is uncertain who is a catechumen, and who a believer: they all have access equally, they listen equally, they pray equally—even pagans, if any happen to come. . . . They also share the kiss of peace with all who come, for they do not care how differently they treat topics, if they meet together to storm the citadel of the one only truth. . . . *All* of them are arrogant . . . *all* offer you *gnosis!* [68]

The principle of equal access, equal participation, and equal claims to knowledge certainly impressed Tertullian. But he took this as evidence that the heretics "overthrow discipline": proper discipline, in his view, required certain degrees of distinction between community members. Tertullian protests especially the participation of "those women among the heretics" who shared with men positions of authority: "They teach, they engage in discussion; they exorcise; they cure" [69]—he suspects that they might even baptize, which meant that they also acted as bishops!

Tertullian also objected to the fact that

> their ordinations are carelessly administered, capricious, and changeable. At one time they put novices in office; at another, persons bound by secular employment. . . . Nowhere is promotion easier than in the camp of rebels, where even the mere fact of being there is a foremost service. So today one man is bishop and tomorrow another; the person

who is a deacon today, tomorrow is a reader; the one who
is a priest today is a layman tomorrow; for even on the
laity they impose the functions of priesthood![70]

This remarkable passage reveals what distinctions Tertullian
considered essential to church order—distinctions between new-
comers and experienced Christians; between women and men;
between a professional clergy and people occupied with secular
employment; between readers, deacons, priests, and bishops—
and above all, between the clergy and the laity. Valentinian
Christians, on the other hand, followed a practice which insured
the equality of all participants. Their system allowed no hierarchy
to form, and no fixed "orders" of clergy. Since each person's role
changed every day, occasions for envy against prominent persons
were minimized.

How was the bishop who defined his role in traditional
Roman terms, as ruler, teacher, and judge of the church, to
respond to this gnostic critique? Irenaeus saw that he, as bishop,
had been placed in a double-bind situation. Certain members of
his flock had been meeting without his authority in private
sessions; Marcus, a self-appointed leader, whom Irenaeus derides
as an "adept in magical impostures,"[71] had initiated them into
secret sacraments and had encouraged them to ignore the bishop's
moral warnings. Contrary to his orders, he says, they did eat
meat sacrificed to idols; they freely attended pagan festivals, and
they violated his strict warnings concerning sexual abstinence
and monogamy.[72] What Irenaeus found most galling of all was
that, instead of repenting or even openly defying the bishop,
they responded to his protests with diabolically clever *theological*
arguments:

> They call [us] "unspiritual," "common," and "ecclesi-
> astic." . . . Because we do not accept their monstrous
> allegations, they say that we go on living in the hebdomad
> [the lower regions], as if we could not lift our minds to the
> things on high, nor understand the things that are above.[73]

Irenaeus was outraged at their claim that they, being spiritual, were released from the ethical restraints that he, as a mere servant of the demiurge, ignorantly sought to foist upon them.[74]

To defend the church against these self-styled theologians, Irenaeus realized that he must forge theological weapons. He believed that if he could demolish the heretical teaching of "another God besides the creator," he could destroy the possibility of ignoring or defying—on allegedly theological grounds —the authority of the "one catholic church" and of its bishop. Like his opponents, Irenaeus took for granted the correlation between the structure of divine authority and human authority in the church. If God is One, then there can be only one true church, and only one representative of the God in the community—the bishop.

Irenaeus declared, therefore, that orthodox Christians must believe above all that God is One—creator, Father, lord, and judge. He warned that it is this one God who established the catholic church, and who "presides with those who exercise moral discipline"[75] within it. Yet he found it difficult to argue theology with the gnostics: they claimed to agree with everything he said, but he knew that secretly they discounted his words as coming from someone unspiritual. So he felt impelled to end his treatise with a solemn call to judgment:

> Let those persons who blaspheme the Creator . . . as
> [do] the Valentinians and all the falsely so-called "gnostics,"
> be recognized as agents of Satan by all who worship God.
> Through their agency Satan even now . . . has been seen to
> speak against God, that God who has prepared eternal fire
> for every kind of apostasy.[76]

But we would be wrong to assume that this struggle involves only members of the laity claiming charismatic inspiration, contending against an organized, spiritless hierarchy of priests and bishops. Irenaeus clearly indicates the opposite. Many whom he censured for propagating gnostic teaching were themselves prominent members of the church hierarchy. In one case Irenaeus wrote to Victor, Bishop of Rome, to warn him that certain gnostic writings were circulating among his congregations.[77] He considered these writings especially dangerous because their author, Florinus, claimed the prestige of being a priest. Yet Irenaeus warns Victor that this priest is also, secretly, a gnostic initiate. Irenaeus warned his own congregations that "those whom many believe to be priests, . . . but who do not place the *fear of God* supreme in their hearts . . . are full of pride at their prominence in the community." Such persons, he explained, are secretly gnostics, who "do evil deeds in secret, saying, 'No one sees us.' "[78] Irenaeus makes clear that he intended to expose those who outwardly acted like orthodox Christians, but who were privately members of gnostic circles.

How could the ordinary Christian tell the difference between true and false priests? Irenaeus declares that those who are orthodox will follow the lines of apostolic succession:

> One must obey the priests who are in the church—that is . . . those who possess the succession from the apostles. For they receive simultaneously with the episcopal succession the sure gift of truth.[79]

The heretics, he explains, depart from common tradition and meet without the bishop's approval:

> One must hold in suspicion others who depart from the primitive succession, and assemble themselves in any place at all. These one must recognize as heretics . . . or as schismatics . . . or as hypocrites. All of these have fallen from the truth.[80]

Irenaeus is pronouncing a solemn episcopal judgment. The gnostics claim to have two sources of tradition, one open, the other secret. Irenaeus ironically agrees with them that there *are* two sources of tradition—but, he declares, as God is one, only one of these derives from God—that is the one the church receives through Christ and his chosen apostles, especially Peter. The other comes from Satan—and goes back to the gnostic teacher Simon Magus (literally, "magician"), Peter's archenemy, who tried to buy the apostle's spiritual power and earned his curse. As Peter heads the true succession, so Simon epitomizes the false, demon-inspired succession of the heretics; he is the "father of all heresies":

> All those who in any way corrupt the truth, and harm the teaching of the church, are the disciples and successors of Simon Magus of Samaria. . . . They put forth, indeed, the name of Jesus Christ as a kind of lure, but in many ways they introduce the impieties of Simon . . . spreading to their hearers the bitter and malignant poison of the great serpent (Satan), the great author of apostasy.[81]

Finally he warns that "some who are considered to be among the orthodox"[82] have much to fear in the coming judgment unless (and this is his main practical point) they now repent, repudiate the teaching of "another God," and submit themselves to the bishop, accepting the "advance discipline"[83] that he will administer to spare them eternal damnation.

Were Irenaeus' religious convictions nothing but political tenets in disguise? Or, conversely, were his politics subordinate to his religious beliefs? Either of these interpretations over-simplifies the situation. Irenaeus' religious convictions and his position—like those of his gnostic opponents—reciprocally influenced one another. If certain gnostics opposed the development of church hierarchy, we need not reduce gnosticism to a political movement that arose in reaction to that development. Followers of Valentinus shared a religious vision of the nature of God that they found incompatible with the rule of priests and bishops that was emerging in the catholic church—and so they resisted it. Irenaeus' religious convictions, conversely, coincided with the structure of the church he defended.

This case is far from unique: we can see throughout the history of Christianity how varying beliefs about the nature of God inevitably bear different political implications. Martin Luther, more than 1,300 years later, felt impelled by his own religious experience and his transformed understanding of God to challenge practices endorsed by his superiors in the Catholic Church, and finally to reject its entire papal and priestly system. George Fox, the radical visionary who founded the Quaker movement, was moved by his encounter with the "inner light" to denounce the whole structure of Puritan authority—legal, governmental, and religious. Paul Tillich proclaimed the doctrine of "God beyond God" as he criticized both Protestant and Catholic churches along with nationalistic and fascist governments.

As the doctrine of Christ's bodily resurrection establishes the initial framework for clerical authority, so the doctrine of the "one God" confirms, for orthodox Christians, the emerging institution of the "one bishop" as monarch ("sole ruler") of the church. We may not be surprised, then, to discover next how the orthodox description of God (as "Father Almighty," for example) serves to define who is included—and who excluded—from participation in the power of priests and bishops.

CHAPTER
III

God the Father/
God the Mother

U NLIKE MANY of his contemporaries among the deities of the ancient Near East, the God of Israel shared his power with no female divinity, nor was he the divine Husband or Lover of any.[1] He can scarcely be characterized in any but masculine epithets: king, lord, master, judge, and father.[2] Indeed, the absence of feminine symbolism for God marks Judaism, Christianity, and Islam in striking contrast to the world's other religious traditions, whether in Egypt, Babylonia, Greece, and Rome, or in Africa, India, and North America, which abound in feminine symbolism. Jewish, Christian, and Islamic theologians today are quick to point out that God is not to be considered in sexual terms at all.[3] Yet the actual language they use daily in worship and prayer conveys a different message: who, growing up with Jewish or Christian tradition, has escaped the distinct impression that God is *masculine*? And while Catholics revere Mary as the mother of Jesus, they never identify her as divine in her own right: if she is "mother of God," she is not "God the Mother" on an equal footing with God the Father!

Christianity, of course, added the trinitarian terms to the Jewish description of God. Yet of the three divine "Persons," two—the Father and the Son—are described in masculine terms, and the third—the Spirit—suggests the sexlessness of the Greek neuter term for spirit, *pneuma*. Whoever investigates the early history of Christianity (the field called "patristics"—that is, study of "the fathers of the church") will be prepared for the passage that concludes the *Gospel of Thomas*:

> Simon Peter said to them [the disciples]: "Let Mary leave us, for women are not worthy of Life." Jesus said, "I myself shall lead her, in order to make her male, so that she too may become a living spirit, resembling you males. For every woman who will make herself male will enter the Kingdom of Heaven."[4]

Strange as it sounds, this simply states what religious rhetoric assumes: that the men form the legitimate body of the community, while women are allowed to participate only when they assimilate themselves to men. Other texts discovered at Nag Hammadi demonstrate one striking difference between these "heretical" sources and orthodox ones: gnostic sources continually use sexual symbolism to describe God. One might expect that these texts would show the influence of archaic pagan traditions of the Mother Goddess, but for the most part, their language is specifically Christian, unmistakably related to a Jewish heritage. Yet instead of describing a monistic and masculine God, many of these texts speak of God as a dyad who embraces both masculine and feminine elements.

One group of gnostic sources claims to have received a secret tradition from Jesus through James and through Mary Magdalene. Members of this group prayed to both the divine Father and Mother: "From Thee, Father, and through Thee, Mother, the two immortal names, Parents of the divine being, and thou, dweller in heaven, humanity, of the mighty name . . ."[5] Other texts indicate that their authors had wondered to whom a single, masculine God proposed, "Let us make man [*adam*] in our image, after our likeness" (Genesis 1:26). Since the Genesis account goes on to say that humanity was created "male and

[49]

female" (1:27), some concluded that the God in whose image we are made must also be both masculine and feminine—both Father and Mother.

How do these texts characterize the divine Mother? I find no simple answer, since the texts themselves are extremely diverse. Yet we may sketch out three primary characterizations. In the first place, several gnostic groups describe the divine Mother as part of an original couple. Valentinus, the teacher and poet, begins with the premise that God is essentially indescribable. But he suggests that the divine can be imagined as a dyad; consisting, in one part, of the Ineffable, the Depth, the Primal Father; and, in the other, of Grace, Silence, the Womb and "Mother of the All."[6] Valentinus reasons that Silence is the appropriate complement of the Father, designating the former as feminine and the latter as masculine because of the grammatical gender of the Greek words. He goes on to describe how Silence receives, as in a womb, the seed of the Ineffable Source; from this she brings forth all the emanations of divine being, ranged in harmonious pairs of masculine and feminine energies.

Followers of Valentinus prayed to her for protection as the Mother, and as "the mystical, eternal Silence."[7] For example, Marcus the magician invokes her as Grace (in Greek, the feminine term *charis*): "May She who is before all things, the incomprehensible and indescribable Grace, fill you within, and increase in you her own knowledge."[8] In his secret celebration of the mass, Marcus teaches that the wine symbolizes her blood. As the cup of wine is offered, he prays that "Grace may flow"[9] into all who drink of it. A prophet and visionary, Marcus calls himself the *"womb* and *recipient* of Silence"[10] (as she is of the Father). The visions he received of the divine being appeared, he reports, in female form.

Another gnostic writing, called the *Great Announcement*, quoted by Hippolytus in his *Refutation of All Heresies*, explains the origin of the universe as follows: From the power of Silence appeared "a great power, the Mind of the Universe, which man-

ages all things, and is a male . . . the other . . . a great Intelligence
. . . is a female which produces all things."[11] Following the
gender of the Greek words for "mind" (*nous*—masculine) and
"intelligence" (*epinoia*—feminine), this author explains that
these powers, joined in union, "are discovered to be duality . . .
This is Mind in Intelligence, and these are separable from one
another, and yet are one, found in a state of duality." This
means, the gnostic teacher explains, that

> there is in everyone [divine power] existing in a latent
> condition . . . This is one power divided above and below;
> generating itself, making itself grow, seeking itself, finding
> itself, being mother of itself, father of itself, sister of itself,
> spouse of itself, daughter of itself, son of itself—mother,
> father, unity, being a source of the entire circle of ex-
> istence.[12]

How did these gnostics intend their meaning to be understood? Different teachers disagreed. Some insisted that the divine
is to be considered masculofeminine—the "great male-female
power." Others claimed that the terms were meant only as
metaphors, since, in reality, the divine is neither male nor
female.[13] A third group suggested that one can describe the
primal Source in either masculine or feminine terms, depending
on which aspect one intends to stress. Proponents of these diverse
views agreed that the divine is to be understood in terms of a
harmonious, dynamic relationship of opposites—a concept that
may be akin to the Eastern view of *yin* and *yang*, but remains
alien to orthodox Judaism and Christianity.

A second characterization of the divine Mother describes her
as Holy Spirit. The *Apocryphon of John* relates how John went
out after the crucifixion with "great grief" and had a mystical
vision of the Trinity. As John was grieving, he says that

> the [heavens were opened and the whole] creation [which
> is] under heaven shone and [the world] trembled. [And I
> was afraid, and I] saw in the light . . . a likeness with
> multiple forms . . . and the likeness had three forms.[14]

To John's question the vision answers: "He said to me, 'John, Jo[h]n, why do you doubt, and why are you afraid? . . . I am the one who [is with you] always. I [am the Father]; I am the Mother; I am the Son.'"[15] This gnostic description of God—as Father, Mother and Son—may startle us at first, but on reflection, we can recognize it as another version of the Trinity. The Greek terminology for the Trinity, which includes the neuter term for spirit (*pneuma*) virtually requires that the third "Person" of the Trinity be asexual. But the author of the *Secret Book* has in mind the Hebrew term for spirit, *ruah*, a feminine word; and so concludes that the feminine "Person" conjoined with the Father and Son must be the Mother. The *Secret Book* goes on to describe the divine Mother:

> . . . (She is) . . . the image of the invisible, virginal, perfect spirit . . . She became the Mother of everything, for she existed before them all, the mother-father [*matropater*] . . .[16]

The *Gospel to the Hebrews* likewise has Jesus speak of "my Mother, the Spirit."[17] In the *Gospel of Thomas*, Jesus contrasts his earthly parents, Mary and Joseph, with his divine Father— the Father of Truth—and his divine Mother, the Holy Spirit. The author interprets a puzzling saying of Jesus' from the New Testament ("Whoever does not hate his father and his mother cannot be my disciple") by adding that "my (earthly) mother [gave me death], but [my] true [Mother] gave me life."[18] So, according to the *Gospel of Philip*, whoever becomes a Christian gains "both father and mother"[19] for the Spirit (*ruah*) is "Mother of many."[20]

A work attributed to the gnostic teacher Simon Magus suggests a mystical meaning for Paradise, the place where human life began:

> Grant Paradise to be the womb; for Scripture teaches us that this is a true assumption when it says, "I am He that formed thee in thy mother's womb" (Isaiah 44:2) . . . Moses . . . using allegory had declared Paradise to be the womb . . . and Eden, the placenta . . .[21]

The river that flows forth from Eden symbolizes the navel, which nourishes the fetus. Simon claims that the Exodus, consequently, signifies the passage out of the womb, and that "the crossing of the Red Sea refers to the blood." Sethian gnostics explain that

> heaven and earth have a shape similar to the womb . . . and if . . . anyone wants to investigate this, let him carefully examine the pregnant womb of any living creature, and he will discover an image of the heavens and the earth.[22]

Evidence for such views, declares Marcus, comes directly from "the cry of the newborn," a spontaneous cry of praise for "the glory of the primal being, in which the powers above are in harmonious embrace."[23]

If some gnostic sources suggest that the Spirit constitutes the maternal element of the Trinity, the *Gospel of Philip* makes an equally radical suggestion about the doctrine that later developed as the virgin birth. Here again, the Spirit is both Mother and Virgin, the counterpart—and consort—of the Heavenly Father: "Is it permitted to utter a mystery? The Father of everything united with the virgin who came down"[24] —that is, with the Holy Spirit descending into the world. But because this process is to be understood symbolically, not literally, the Spirit remains a virgin. The author goes on to explain that as "Adam came into being from two virgins, from the Spirit and from the virgin earth" so "Christ, therefore, was born from a virgin"[25] (that is, from the Spirit). But the author ridicules those literal-minded Christians who mistakenly refer the virgin birth to Mary, Jesus' mother, as though she conceived apart from Joseph: "They do not know what they are saying. When did a woman ever conceive by a woman?"[26] Instead, he argues, virgin birth refers to that mysterious union of the two divine powers, the Father of All and the Holy Spirit.

In addition to the eternal, mystical Silence and the Holy Spirit, certain gnostics suggest a third characterization of the divine Mother: as Wisdom. Here the Greek feminine term for "wisdom," *sophia*, translates a Hebrew feminine term, *hokhmah*. Early interpreters had pondered the meaning of certain Biblical passages—for example, the saying in Proverbs that "God made the world in Wisdom." Could Wisdom be the feminine power in which God's creation was "conceived"? According to one teacher, the double meaning of the term conception—physical and intellectual—suggests this possibility: "The image of thought [*ennoia*] is feminine, since . . . [it] is a power of conception."[27] The *Apocalypse of Adam*, discovered at Nag Hammadi, tells of a feminine power who wanted to conceive by herself:

> . . . from the nine Muses, one separated away. She came to a high mountain and spent time seated there, so that she desired herself alone in order to become androgynous. She fulfilled her desire, and became pregnant from her desire . . .[28]

The poet Valentinus uses this theme to tell a famous myth about Wisdom: Desiring to conceive by herself, apart from her masculine counterpart, she succeeded, and became the "great creative power from whom all things originate," often called Eve, "Mother of all living." But since her desire violated the harmonious union of opposites intrinsic in the nature of created being, what she produced was aborted and defective;[29] from this, says Valentinus, originated the terror and grief that mar human existence.[30] To shape and manage her creation, Wisdom brought forth the demiurge, the creator-God of Israel, as her agent.[31]

Wisdom, then, bears several connotations in gnostic sources. Besides being the "first universal creator,"[32] who brings forth all creatures, she also enlightens human beings and makes them wise. Followers of Valentinus and Marcus therefore prayed to the Mother as the "mystical, eternal Silence" and to "Grace, She who is before all things," and as "incorruptible Wisdom"[33] for insight (*gnosis*). Other gnostics attributed to her the benefits that Adam and Eve received in Paradise. First, she taught them self-awareness; second, she guided them to find food; third, she assisted in the conception of their third and fourth children, who were, according to this account, their third son, Seth, and their

first daughter, Norea.[34] Even more: when the creator became
angry with the human race

> because they did not worship or honor him as Father and
> God, he sent forth a flood upon them, that he might destroy
> them all. But Wisdom opposed him . . . and Noah and his
> family were saved in the ark by means of the sprinkling of
> the light that proceeded from her, and through it the world
> was again filled with humankind.[35]

Another newly discovered text from Nag Hammadi,
Trimorphic Protennoia (literally, the "Triple-formed Primal
Thought"), celebrates the feminine powers of Thought, Intel-
ligence, and Foresight. The text opens as a divine figure speaks:

> [I] am [Protennoia the] Thought that [dwells] in [the
> Light]. . . . [she who exists] before the All . . . I move in
> every creature. . . . I am the Invisible One within the All.[36]

She continues: "I am perception and knowledge, uttering a Voice
by means of Thought. [I] am the real Voice. I cry out in everyone, and they know that a seed dwells within."[37] The second
section, spoken by a second divine figure, opens with the words

> I am the Voice . . . [It is] I [who] speak within every
> creature . . . Now I have come a second time in the likeness
> of a female, and have spoken with them. . . . I have revealed
> myself in the Thought of the likeness of my masculinity.[38]

Later the voice explains:

> I am androgynous. [I am both Mother and] Father,
> since [I copulate] with myself . . . [and with those who
> love] me . . . I am the Womb [that gives shape] to the All
> . . . I am Me[iroth]ea, the glory of the Mother.[39]

Even more remarkable is the gnostic poem called the
Thunder, Perfect Mind. This text contains a revelation spoken
by a feminine power:

> I am the first and the last. I am the honored one and the
> scorned one. I am the whore, and the holy one. I am the

wife and the virgin. I am ⟨the mother⟩ and the daughter.
. . . I am she whose wedding is great, and I have not taken
a husband. . . . I am knowledge, and ignorance. . . . I am
shameless; I am ashamed. I am strength, and I am fear. . . . I
am foolish, and I am wise. . . . I am godless, and I am one
whose God is great.[40]

What does the use of such symbolism imply for the understanding of human nature? One text, having previously described
the divine Source as a "bisexual Power," goes on to say that
"what came into being from that Power—that is, humanity,
being one—is discovered to be two: a male-female being that
bears the female within it."[41] This refers to the story of Eve's
"birth" out of Adam's side (so that Adam, being one, is "discovered to be two," an androgyne who "bears the female within
him"). Yet this reference to the creation story of Genesis 2 (an
account which inverts the biological birth process, and so
attributes to the male the creative function of the female) is
unusual in gnostic sources. More often, gnostic writers refer to
the first creation account in Genesis 1:26–27 ("Then God said,
Let us make man [adam] in our image, after our likeness . . . in
the image of God he created him; male and female he created
them"). Rabbis in Talmudic times knew a Greek version of the
passage that suggested to Rabbi Samuel bar Nachman, influenced
by Plato's myth of androgyny, that

> when the Holy one . . . first created mankind, he created
> him with two faces, two sets of genitals, four arms and legs,
> back to back. Then he split Adam in two, and made two
> backs, one on each side.[42]

Some gnostics adopted this idea, teaching that Genesis 1:26–27
narrates an androgynous creation. Marcus (whose prayer to the
Mother is given above) not only concludes from this account
that God is dyadic ("Let us make humanity") but also that
"humanity, which was formed according to the image and likeness of God (Father and Mother) was masculo-feminine."[43] His
contemporary, the gnostic Theodotus (c. 160), explains that the

saying "according to the image of God he made them, male and female he made them," means that "the male and female elements together constitute the finest production of the Mother, Wisdom."[44] Gnostic sources which describe God as a dyad whose nature includes both masculine and feminine elements often give a similar description of human nature.

Yet all the sources cited so far—secret gospels, revelations, mystical teachings—are among those not included in the select list that constitutes the New Testament collection. Every one of the secret texts which gnostic groups revered was omitted from the canonical collection, and branded as heretical by those who called themselves orthodox Christians. By the time the process of sorting the various writings ended—probably as late as the year 200—virtually all the feminine imagery for God had disappeared from orthodox Christian tradition.

What is the reason for this total rejection? The gnostics themselves asked this question of their orthodox opponents and pondered it among themselves. Some concluded that the God of Israel himself initiated the polemics which his followers carried out in his name. For, they argued, this creator was a derivative, merely instrumental power whom the Mother had created to administer the universe, but his own self-conception was far more grandiose. They say that he believed that he had made everything by himself, but that, in reality, he had created the world because Wisdom, his Mother, "infused him with energy" and implanted into him her own ideas. But he was foolish, and acted unconsciously, unaware that the ideas he used came from her; "he was even ignorant of his own Mother."[45] Followers of Valentinus suggested that the Mother Herself had encouraged the God of Israel to think that he was acting autonomously, but, as they explain, "It was because he was foolish and ignorant of his Mother that he said, 'I am God; there is none beside me.'"[46] According to another account, the creator caused his Mother to grieve by creating inferior beings, so she left him alone and withdrew into the upper regions of the heavens. "Since she had departed, he imagined that he was the only being in existence;

and therefore he declared, 'I am a jealous God, and besides me there is no one.' "[47] Others agree in attributing to him this more sinister motive—jealousy. According to the *Secret Book of John*:

> . . . he said . . . , "I am a jealous God, and there is no other God beside me." But by announcing this he indicated to the angels . . . that another God does exist; for if there were no other one, of whom would he be jealous? . . . Then the mother began to be distressed.[48]

Others declared that his Mother refused to tolerate such presumption:

> [The creator], becoming arrogant in spirit, boasted himself over all those things that were below him, and exclaimed, "I am father, and God, and above me there is no one." But his mother, hearing him speak thus, cried out against him, "Do not lie, Ialdabaoth . . ."[49]

Often, in these gnostic texts, the creator is castigated for his arrogance—nearly always by a superior feminine power. According to the *Hypostasis of the Archons*, discovered at Nag Hammadi, both the mother and her daughter objected when

> he became arrogant, saying, "It is I who am God, and there is no other apart from me." . . . And a voice came forth from above the realm of absolute power, saying, "You are wrong, Samael" [which means, "god of the blind"]. And he said, "If any other thing exists before me, let it appear to me!" And immediately, Sophia ("Wisdom") stretched forth her finger, and introduced light into matter, and she followed it down into the region of Chaos. . . . And he again said to his offspring, "It is I who am the God of All." And Life, the daughter of Wisdom, cried out; she said to him, "You are wrong, Saklas!"[50]

The gnostic teacher Justinus describes the Lord's shock, terror, and anxiety "when he discovered that he was not the God of the universe." Gradually his shock gave way to wonder, and finally he came to welcome what Wisdom had taught him. The teacher concludes: "This is the meaning of the saying, 'The fear of the Lord is the beginning of Wisdom.' "[51]

Yet all of these are mythical explanations. Can we find any actual, historical reasons why these gnostic writings were suppressed? This raises a much larger question: By what means, and for what reasons, did certain ideas come to be classified as heretical, and others as orthodox, by the beginning of the third century? We may find one clue to the answer if we ask whether gnostic Christians derive any practical, social consequences from their conception of God—and of humanity—in terms that included the feminine element. Here, clearly, the answer is *yes*.

Bishop Irenaeus notes with dismay that women especially are attracted to heretical groups. "Even in our own district of the Rhône valley," he admits, the gnostic teacher Marcus had attracted "many foolish women" from his own congregation, including the wife of one of Irenaeus' own deacons.[52] Professing himself to be at a loss to account for the attraction that Marcus' group held, he offers only one explanation: that Marcus himself was a diabolically clever seducer, a magician who compounded special aphrodisiacs to "deceive, victimize, and defile" his prey. Whether his accusations have any factual basis no one knows. But when he describes Marcus' techniques of seduction, Irenaeus indicates that he is speaking metaphorically. For, he says, Marcus "addresses them in such seductive words" as his prayers to Grace, "She who is before all things,"[53] and to Wisdom and Silence, the feminine element of the divine being. Second, he says, Marcus seduced women "by telling them to prophesy"[54]— which they were strictly forbidden to do in the orthodox church. When he initiated a woman, Marcus concluded the initiation prayer with the words "Behold, Grace has come upon you; open your mouth, and prophesy."[55] Then, as the bishop indignantly describes it, Marcus' "deluded victim . . . impudently utters some nonsense," and "henceforth considers herself to be a prophet!" Worst of all, from Irenaeus' viewpoint, Marcus invited women to act as priests in celebrating the eucharist with him: he "hands the cups to women"[56] to offer up the eucharistic prayer, and to pronounce the words of consecration.

Tertullian expresses similar outrage at such acts of gnostic Christians:

> These heretical women—how audacious they are! They have no modesty; they are bold enough to teach, to engage in argument, to enact exorcisms, to undertake cures, and, it may be, even to baptize![57]

Tertullian directed another attack against "that viper"[58]—a woman teacher who led a congregation in North Africa. He himself agreed with what he called the "precepts of ecclesiastical discipline concerning women," which specified:

> It is not permitted for a woman to speak in the church, nor is it permitted for her to teach, nor to baptize, nor to offer [the eucharist], nor to claim for herself a share in any *masculine* function—not to mention any priestly office.[59]

One of Tertullian's prime targets, the heretic Marcion, had, in fact, scandalized his orthodox contemporaries by appointing women on an equal basis with men as priests and bishops. The gnostic teacher Marcellina traveled to Rome to represent the Carpocratian group,[60] which claimed to have received secret teaching from Mary, Salome, and Martha. The Montanists, a radical prophetic circle, honored two women, Prisca and Maximilla, as founders of the movement.

Our evidence, then, clearly indicates a correlation between religious theory and social practice.[61] Among such gnostic groups as the Valentinians, women were considered equal to men; some were revered as prophets; others acted as teachers, traveling evangelists, healers, priests, perhaps even bishops. This general observation is not, however, universally applicable. At least three heretical circles that retained a masculine image of God included women who took positions of leadership—the Marcionites, the Montanists, and the Carpocratians. But from the year 200, we have no evidence for women taking prophetic, priestly, and episcopal roles among orthodox churches.

This is an extraordinary development, considering that in its earliest years the Christian movement showed a remarkable openness toward women. Jesus himself violated Jewish convention by talking openly with women, and he included them among his companions. Even the gospel of Luke in the New Testament tells his reply when Martha, his hostess, complains to him that she is doing housework alone while her sister Mary sits listening to him: "Do you not care that my sister has left me to serve alone? Tell her, then, to help me." But instead of supporting her, Jesus chides Martha for taking upon herself so many anxieties, declaring that "one thing is needful: Mary has chosen the good portion, which shall not be taken away from her."[62] Some ten to twenty years after Jesus' death, certain women held positions of leadership in local Christian groups; women acted as prophets, teachers, and evangelists. Professor Wayne Meeks suggests that, at Christian initiation, the person presiding ritually announced that "in Christ . . . there is neither male nor female."[63] Paul quotes this saying, and endorses the work of women he recognizes as deacons and fellow workers; he even greets one, apparently, as an outstanding apostle, senior to himself in the movement.[64]

Yet Paul also expresses ambivalence concerning the practical implications of human equality. Discussing the public activity of women in the churches, he argues from his own—traditionally Jewish—conception of a monistic, masculine God for a divinely ordained hierarchy of social subordination: as God has authority over Christ, he declares, citing Genesis 2–3, so man has authority over woman:

> . . . a man . . . is the image and glory of God; but woman is the glory of man. (For man was not made from woman, but woman from man. Neither was man created for woman, but woman for man.)[65]

While Paul acknowledged women as his equals "in Christ," and allowed for them a wider range of activity than did traditional

Jewish congregations, he could not bring himself to advocate their equality in social and political terms. Such ambivalence opened the way for the statements found in I Corinthians 14, 34 f., whether written by Paul or inserted by someone else: ". . . the women should keep silence in the churches. For they are not permitted to speak, but they should be subordinate . . . it is shameful for a woman to speak in church."

Such contradictory attitudes toward women reflect a time of social transition, as well as the diversity of cultural influences on churches scattered throughout the known world.[66] In Greece and Asia Minor, women participated with men in religious cults, especially the cults of the Great Mother and of the Egyptian goddess Isis.[67] While the leading roles were reserved for men, women took part in the services and professions. Some women took up education, the arts, and professions such as medicine. In Egypt, women had attained, by the first century A.D., a relatively advanced state of emancipation, socially, politically, and legally. In Rome, forms of education had changed, around 200 B.C., to offer to some children from the aristocracy the same curriculum for girls as for boys. Two hundred years later, at the beginning of the Christian era, the archaic, patriarchal forms of Roman marriage were increasingly giving way to a new legal form in which the man and woman bound themselves to each other with voluntary and mutual vows. The French scholar Jérôme Carcopino, in a discussion entitled "Feminism and Demoralization," explains that by the second century A.D., upper-class women often insisted upon "living their own life."[68] Male satirists complained of their aggressiveness in discussions of literature, mathematics, and philosophy, and ridiculed their enthusiasm for writing poems, plays, and music.[69] Under the Empire,

> women were everywhere involved in business, social life, such as theaters, sports events, concerts, parties, travelling— with or without their husbands. They took part in a whole range of athletics, even bore arms and went to battle . . .[70]

and made major inroads into professional life. Women of the Jewish communities, on the other hand, were excluded from actively participating in public worship, in education, and in social and political life outside the family.[71]

Yet despite all of this, and despite the previous public activity of Christian women, the majority of Christian churches in the second century went with the majority of the middle class in opposing the move toward equality, which found its support primarily in rich or what we would call bohemian circles. By the year 200, the majority of Christian communities endorsed as canonical the pseudo-Pauline letter of Timothy, which stresses (and exaggerates) the antifeminist element in Paul's views: "Let a woman learn in silence with all submissiveness. I permit no woman to teach or to have authority over men; she is to keep silent."[72] Orthodox Christians also accepted as Pauline the letters to the Colossians and to the Ephesians, which order that women "be subject in everything to their husbands."[73]

Clement, Bishop of Rome, writes in his letter to the unruly church in Corinth that women are to "remain in the rule of subjection"[74] to their husbands. While in earlier times Christian men and women sat together for worship, in the middle of the second century—precisely at the time of struggle with gnostic Christians—orthodox communities began to adopt the synagogue custom, segregating women from men.[75] By the end of the second century, women's participation in worship was explicitly condemned: groups in which women continued on to leadership were branded as heretical.

What was the reason for these changes? The scholar Johannes Leipoldt suggests that the influx of many Hellenized Jews into the movement may have influenced the church in the direction of Jewish traditions, but, as he admits, "this is only an attempt to explain the situation: *the reality itself is the only certain thing.*"[76] Professor Morton Smith suggests that the change may have resulted from Christianity's move up in social scale from lower to middle class. He observes that in the lower class, where all labor was needed, women had been allowed to perform any services they could (so today, in the Near East, only middle-class women are veiled).

Both orthodox and gnostic texts suggest that this question proved to be explosively controversial. Antagonists on both sides resorted to the polemical technique of writing literature that allegedly derived from apostolic times, professing to give the original apostles' views on the subject. As noted before, the *Gospel of Philip* tells of rivalry between the male disciples and Mary Magdalene, here described as Jesus' most intimate companion, the symbol of divine Wisdom:

> . . . the companion of the [Savior is] Mary Magdalene. [But Christ loved] her more than [all] the disciples and used to kiss her [often] on her [mouth]. The rest of [the disciples were offended by it . . .]. They said to him, "Why do you love her more than all of us?" The Savior answered and said to them, "Why do I not love you as [I love] her?"⁷⁷

The *Dialogue of the Savior* not only includes Mary Magdalene as one of three disciples chosen to receive special teaching but also praises her above the other two, Thomas and Matthew: ". . . she spoke as a woman who knew the All."⁷⁸

Other secret texts use the figure of Mary Magdalene to suggest that women's activity challenged the leaders of the orthodox community, who regarded Peter as their spokesman. The *Gospel of Mary* relates that when the disciples, disheartened and terrified after the crucifixion, asked Mary to encourage them by telling them what the Lord had told her secretly, she agrees, and teaches them until Peter, furious, asks, "Did he really speak privately with a woman, (and) not openly to us? Are we to turn about and all listen to her? Did he prefer her to us?" Distressed at his rage, Mary replies, "My brother Peter, what do you think? Do you think that I thought this up myself in my heart, or that I am lying about the Savior?" Levi breaks in at this point to mediate the dispute: "Peter, you have always been hot-tempered. Now I see you contending against the woman like the adversaries. But if the Savior made her worthy, who are you, indeed, to reject her? Surely the Lord knew her very well. That is why he loved her more than us."⁷⁹ Then the others agree to accept Mary's teaching, and, encouraged by her words, go out to preach. Another argument between Peter and Mary occurs in *Pistis Sophia* ("Faith Wisdom"). Peter complains that Mary is dominating the conversation with Jesus and displacing the rightful priority of Peter and his brother apostles. He urges Jesus to silence her and is quickly rebuked. Later, however, Mary admits to Jesus that she hardly dares speak to him freely because, in her words, "Peter makes me hesitate; I am afraid of him, because he hates the female race."⁸⁰ Jesus replies that whoever the Spirit inspires is divinely ordained to speak, whether man or woman.

Orthodox Christians retaliated with alleged "apostolic" letters and dialogues that make the opposite point. The most famous examples are, of course, the pseudo-Pauline letters cited above. In I and II Timothy, Colossians, and Ephesians, "Paul" insists that women be subordinate to men. The letter of Titus, in Paul's name, directs the selection of bishops in terms that entirely exclude women from consideration. Literally and figuratively, the bishop is to be a father figure to the congregation. He must be a man whose wife and children are "submissive [to him] in every way"; this proves his ability to keep "God's church"⁸¹ in order, and its members properly subordinated. Before the end of the second century, the *Apostolic Church Order* appeared in orthodox communities. Here the apostles are depicted discussing controversial questions. With Mary and Martha present, John says,

> When the Master blessed the bread and the cup and signed them with the words, "This is my body and blood," he did not offer it to the women who are with us. Martha said, "He did not offer it to Mary, because he saw her laugh." Mary said, "I no longer laugh; he said to us before, as he taught, 'Your weakness is redeemed through strength.' "⁸²

But her argument fails; the male disciples agree that, for this reason, no woman shall be allowed to become a priest.

We can see, then, two very different patterns of sexual attitudes emerging in orthodox and gnostic circles. In simplest form, many gnostic Christians correlate their description of God in both masculine and feminine terms with a complementary description of human nature. Most often they refer to the creation account of Genesis 1, which suggests an equal or androgynous human creation. Gnostic Christians often take the principle of equality between men and women into the social and political structures of their communities. The orthodox pattern is strikingly different: it describes God in exclusively masculine terms, and typically refers to Genesis 2 to describe how Eve was created from Adam, and for his fulfillment. Like the gnostic view, this translates into social practice: by the late second century, the orthodox community came to accept the domination of men over women as the divinely ordained order, not only for social and family life, but also for the Christian churches.

Yet exceptions to these patterns do occur. Gnostics were not unanimous in affirming women—nor were the orthodox unanimous in denigrating them. Certain gnostic texts undeniably speak of the feminine in terms of contempt. The *Book of Thomas the Contender* addresses men with the warning "Woe to you who love intimacy with womankind, and polluted intercourse with it!"[83] The *Paraphrase of Shem*, also from Nag Hammadi, describes the horror of Nature, who "turned her dark vagina and cast from her the power of fire, which was in her from the beginning, through the practice of darkness."[84] According to the *Dialogue of the Savior*, Jesus warns his disciples to "pray in the place where there is no woman," and to "destroy the works of femaleness . . ."[85]

Yet in each of these cases the target is not woman, but the power of sexuality. In the *Dialogue of the Savior*, for example, Mary Magdalene, praised as "the woman who knew the All," stands among the three disciples who receive Jesus' commands: she, along with Judas and Matthew, rejects the "works of femaleness"—that is, apparently, the activities of intercourse and procreation.[86] These sources show that some extremists in the gnostic movement agreed with certain radical feminists who today insist that only those who renounce sexual activity can achieve human equality and spiritual greatness.

Other gnostic sources reflect the assumption that the status of a man is superior to that of a woman. Nor need this surprise us; as language comes from social experience, any of these writers, whether man or woman, Roman, Greek, Egyptian, or Jewish, would have learned this elementary lesson from his or her social experience. Some gnostics, reasoning that as *man* surpasses *woman* in ordinary existence, so the *divine* surpasses the *human*, transform the terms into metaphor. The puzzling saying attributed to Jesus in the *Gospel of Thomas*—that Mary must become male in order to become a "living spirit, resembling you males. For every woman who will make herself male will enter the Kingdom of Heaven"[87]—may be taken symbolically: what is merely human (therefore *female*) must be transformed into what is divine (the "living spirit" the *male*). So, according to other passages in the *Gospel of Thomas*, Salome and Mary become Jesus' disciples when they transcend their human nature, and so "become male."[88] In the *Gospel of Mary*, Mary herself urges the other disciples to "praise his greatness, for he has prepared us, and made us into *men*."[89]

Conversely, we find a striking exception to the orthodox pattern in the writings of one revered father of the church, Clement of Alexandria. Clement, writing in Egypt c. 180, identifies himself as orthodox, although he knows members of gnostic groups and their writings well: some even suggest that he was himself a gnostic initiate. Yet his own works demonstrate how all three elements of what we have called the gnostic pattern could be worked into fully orthodox teaching. First, Clement characterizes God in feminine as well as masculine terms:

> The Word is everything to the child, both father and mother, teacher and nurse . . . The nutriment is the milk of the Father . . . and the Word alone supplies us children with

the milk of love, and only those who suck at this breast are truly happy. For this reason, seeking is called sucking; to those infants who seek the Word, the Father's loving breasts supply milk.[90]

Second, in describing human nature, he insists that

men and women share equally in perfection, and are to receive the same instruction and the same discipline. For the name "humanity" is common to both men and women; and for us "in Christ there is neither male nor female."[91]

As he urges women to participate with men in the community, Clement offers a list—unique in orthodox tradition—of women whose achievements he admires. They range from ancient examples, like Judith, the assassin who destroyed Israel's enemy, to Queen Esther, who rescued her people from genocide, as well as others who took radical political stands. He mentions Arignote the writer, Themisto the Epicurean philosopher, and many other women philosophers, including two who studied with Plato, and one trained by Socrates. Indeed, he cannot contain his praise:

What shall I say? Did not Theano the Pythagorean make such progress in philosophy that when a man, staring at her, said, "Your arm is beautiful," she replied, "Yes, but it is not on public display."[92]

Clement concludes his list with famous women poets and painters.

But Clement's demonstration that even orthodox Christians could affirm the feminine element—and the active participation of women—found little following. His perspective, formed in the cosmopolitan atmosphere of Alexandria and articulated among wealthy and educated members of Egyptian society, may have proved too alien for the majority of Western Christian communities which were scattered from Asia Minor to Greece, Rome, and provincial Africa and Gaul. The majority adopted instead the position of Clement's severe and provincial contemporary, Tertullian:

> It is not permitted for a woman to speak in the church,
> nor is it permitted for her to teach, nor to baptize, nor to
> offer [the eucharist], nor to claim for herself a share in any
> masculine function—least of all, in priestly office.[93]

Their consensus, which ruled out Clement's position, has continued to dominate the majority of Christian churches: nearly 2,000 years later, in 1977, Pope Paul VI, Bishop of Rome, declared that a woman cannot be a priest "because our Lord was a man"! The Nag Hammadi sources, discovered at a time of contemporary social crises concerning sexual roles, challenge us to reinterpret history—and to re-evaluate the present situation.

CHAPTER
IV

The Passion of Christ and the Persecution of Christians

THERE IS ONLY one fact on which nearly all accounts about Jesus of Nazareth, whether written by persons hostile or devoted to him, agree: that, by order of the Roman prefect, Pontius Pilate, he was condemned and crucified (c. 30). Tacitus, the aristocratic Roman historian (c. 55–115), knowing virtually nothing about Jesus, mentions only this. Relating the history of the infamous Nero (emperor 54–58), he says that Nero, accused of starting major fires in Rome,

> substituted as culprits and punished with the utmost refinements of cruelty, a class of persons hated for their vices, whom the crowd called Christians. *Christus, the founder of the name, had undergone the death penalty in the reign of Tiberius, by sentence of the procurator Pontius Pilate*, and the pernicious superstition was checked for a moment, only to break out once more, not only in Judea, the home of the disease, but in the capital itself, where everything horrible or shameful in the world gathers and becomes fashionable.[1]

The Jewish historian Josephus mentions Jesus of Nazareth in a list of troubles that disturbed Jewish relations with Rome when Pilate was governor (roughly 26–36). A comment attributed to Josephus reports that "Pilate, having heard him accused by men of the highest standing among us . . . condemned him to be crucified."[2]

Jesus' followers confirm this report. The gospel of Mark, probably the earliest of the New Testament accounts (c. 70–80), tells how Jesus, betrayed by Judas Iscariot at night in the garden of Gethsemane opposite Jerusalem, was arrested by armed men as his disciples fled.[3] Charged with sedition before Pilate, he was condemned to death.[4] Crucified, Jesus lived for several hours before, as Mark tells it, he "uttered a loud cry"[5] and died. The gospels of Luke and John, written perhaps a generation later (c. 90–110), describe his death in more heroic terms: Jesus forgives his torturers, and, with a prayer, yields up his life.[6] Yet all four of the New Testament gospels describe his suffering, death, and hasty burial. The gospels, of course, interpret the circumstances leading to his death to demonstrate his innocence. Mark says that the chief priests and leaders in Jerusalem planned to have Jesus arrested and executed because of his teaching against them.[7] John presents a fuller account, historically plausible. He reports that as Jesus' popularity grew and attracted increasing numbers to his movement, the chief priests gathered the council of the Sanhedrin to discuss the dangers of riot. Some among the uneducated masses already acclaimed Jesus as Messiah[8]—the "anointed king" who they expected would liberate Israel from foreign imperialism and restore the Jewish state. Especially during Passover, when thousands of Jews poured into Jerusalem to celebrate the holiday, this impetus might ignite feelings of Jewish nationalism, already smoldering in the city, into revolt. The council held the responsibility for keeping the peace between the Jewish population and the Roman occupying army—a peace so tenuous that when, only a few years later, a Roman soldier stationed on guard in Jerusalem during Passover expressed his contempt by exposing himself in the Temple courtyard, his act provoked a riot in which 30,000 people are said to have lost their lives. Josephus, who tells this story, adds: "Thus the Feast ended in distress to the whole nation, and bereavement to every household."[9]

John reconstructs the council debate concerning Jesus: "What are we to do? . . . If we let him go on thus," the masses may demonstrate in favor of this alleged new Jewish king, "and the Romans will come and destroy both our holy place and our nation."[10] The chief priest Caiphas argued for the expedience of arresting one man at once, rather than endanger the whole population.[11] Even John had to recognize the political acumen of this reasoning: he wrote his account not long after the Jewish War of 66–70, an insurrection against Rome that ended in the total disaster which, according to John, Caiphas had predicted: the Temple burned to the ground, the city of Jerusalem devastated, the population decimated.

Yet if the sources agree on the basic facts of Jesus' execution, Christians sharply disagree on their interpretation. One gnostic text from Nag Hammadi, the *Apocalypse of Peter*, relates a radically different version of the crucifixion:

> . . . I saw him apparently being seized by them. And I said, "What am I seeing, O Lord? Is it really you whom they take? And are you holding on to me? And are they hammering the feet and hands of another? Who is this one above the cross, who is glad and laughing?" The Savior said to me, "He whom you saw being glad and laughing above the cross is the Living Jesus. But he into whose hands and feet they are driving the nails is his fleshly part, which is the substitute. They put to shame that which remained in his likeness. And look at him, and [look at] me!"[12]

Another of the Nag Hammadi texts, the *Second Treatise of the Great Seth*, relates Christ's teaching that

> it was another . . . who drank the gall and the vinegar; it was not I. They struck me with the reed; it was another, Simon,

who bore the cross on his shoulder. It was another upon whom they placed the crown of thorns. But I was rejoicing in the height over . . . their error . . . And I was laughing at their ignorance.[13]

What does this mean? The *Acts of John*—one of the most famous gnostic texts, and one of the few discovered before Nag Hammadi, having somehow survived, in fragmentary form, repeated denunciations by the orthodox—explains that Jesus was not a human being at all; instead, he was a spiritual being who adapted himself to human perception. The *Acts* tells how James once saw him standing on the shore in the form of a child, but when he pointed him out to John,

> I [John] said, "Which child?" And he answered me, "The one who is beckoning to us." And I said, "This is because of the long watch we have kept at sea. You are not seeing straight, brother James. Do you not see the man standing there who is handsome, fair and cheerful looking?" But he said to me, "I do not see that man, my brother."[14]

Going ashore to investigate, they became even more confused. According to John,

> he appeared to me again as rather bald-⟨headed⟩ but with a thick flowing beard, but to James as a young man whose beard was just beginning. . . . I tried to see him as he was . . . But he sometimes appeared to me as a small man with no good looks, and then again as looking up to heaven.[15]

John continues:

> I will tell you another glory, brethren; sometimes when I meant to touch him I encountered a material, solid body; but at other times again when I felt him, his substance was immaterial and incorporeal . . . as if it did not exist at all.[16]

John adds that he checked carefully for footprints, but Jesus never left any—nor did he ever blink his eyes. All of this demonstrates to John that his nature was spiritual, not human.

The *Acts* goes on to tell how Jesus, anticipating arrest, joined with his disciples in Gethsemane the night before:

> . . . he assembled us all, and said, "Before I am delivered to them, let us sing a hymn to the Father, and so go to meet what lies before (us)." So he told us to form a circle, holding one another's hands, and himself stood in the middle . . .[17]

Instructing the disciples to "Answer Amen to me," he began to intone a mystical chant, which reads, in part,

> "To the Universe belongs the dancer."—"Amen."
> "He who does not dance does not know what happens."— "Amen." . . .
> "Now if you follow my dance, see yourself in Me who am speaking . . .
> You who dance, consider what I do, for yours is
> This passion of Man which I am to suffer. For you could by no means have understood what you suffer
> unless to you as Logos I had been sent by the Father . . .
> Learn how to suffer and you shall be able not to suffer."[18]

John continues:

> After the Lord had danced with us, my beloved, he went out [to suffer]. And we were like men amazed or fast asleep, and we fled this way and that. And so I saw him suffer, and did not wait by his suffering, but fled to the Mount of Olives and wept . . . And when he was hung (upon the Cross) on Friday, at the sixth hour of the day there came a darkness over the whole earth.[19]

At that moment John, sitting in a cave in Gethsemane, suddenly saw a vision of Jesus, who said,

> "John, for the people below . . . I am being crucified and pierced with lances . . . and given vinegar and gall to drink. But to you I am speaking, and listen to what I speak."[20]

Then the vision reveals to John a "cross of light," and explains that "I have suffered none of the things which they will say of me; even that suffering which I showed to you and to the rest in my dance, I will that it be called a mystery."[21] Other gnostics, followers of Valentinus, interpret the meaning of such paradoxes in a different way. According to the *Treatise on Resurrection*, discovered at Nag Hammadi, insofar as Jesus was the "Son of Man," being human, he suffered and died like the rest of humanity.[22] But since he was also "Son of God," the divine spirit within him could not die: in that sense he transcended suffering and death.

Yet orthodox Christians insist that Jesus *was* a human being, and that all "straight-thinking" Christians must take the crucifixion as a historical and literal event. To ensure this they place in the creed, as a central element of faith, the simple statement that "Jesus Christ suffered under Pontius Pilate, was crucified, dead, and buried." Pope Leo the Great (c. 447) condemned such writings as the *Acts of John* as "a hotbed of manifold perversity," which "should not only be forbidden, but entirely destroyed and burned with fire." But because heretical circles continued to copy and hide this text, the second Nicene Council, three hundred years later, had to repeat the judgment, directing that "No one is to copy [this book]: not only so, but we consider that it deserves to be consigned to the fire."

What lies behind this vehemence? Why does faith in the passion and death of Christ become an essential element—some say, *the* essential element—of orthodox Christianity? I am convinced that we cannot answer this question fully until we recognize that controversy over the interpretation of Christ's suffering and death involved, for Christians of the first and second centuries, an urgent practical question: How are believers to respond to persecution, which raises the imminent threat of their *own* suffering and death?

No issue could be more immediate to Jesus' disciples, having themselves experienced the traumatic events of his betrayal and arrest, and having heard accounts of his trial, torture, and final agony. From that time, especially when the most prominent among them, Peter and James, were arrested and executed, every Christian recognized that affiliation with the movement placed him in danger. Both Tacitus and Suetonius, the historian of the imperial court (c. 115), who shared an utter contempt for Christians, mention the group principally as the target of official persecution. In telling the life of Nero, Suetonius reports, in a list of the *good* things the emperor did, that "punishment was inflicted on the Christians, a class of persons given to a new and malificent superstition."[23] Tacitus adds to his remarks on the fire in Rome:

> First, then, those of the sect were arrested who confessed; next, on their disclosures, vast numbers were convicted, not so much on the count of arson, as for hatred of the human race. And ridicule accompanied their end: they were covered with wild beasts' skins and torn to death by dogs; or they were fastened on crosses, and, when daylight failed, were burned to serve as torches by night. Nero had offered his gardens for the spectacle . . .[24]

Tacitus interprets Nero's action in terms of his need for a scapegoat. As yet, the government may have considered the Christians outside Rome—if it considered them at all—too insignificant to initiate systematic action against the movement. But since the time that Augustus ruled as emperor (27 B.C.–A.D. 14), the emperor and the Senate had moved to repress any social dissidents whom they thought potential troublemakers, as they did astrologers, magicians, followers of foreign religious cults, and philosophers.[25] The Christian group bore all the marks of conspiracy. First, they identified themselves as followers of a man accused of magic[26] and executed for that and for treason; second, they were "atheists," who denounced as "demons" the gods who protected the fortunes of the Roman state—even the *genius* (divine spirit) of the emperor himself; third, they belonged to an illegal society. Besides these acts that police could verify, rumor indicated that their secrecy concealed atrocities: their enemies said that they ritually ate human flesh and drank human blood, practices of which magicians were commonly accused.[27] Although at this time no law specifically prohibited conversion to Christianity, any magistrate who heard a person accused of Christianity was required to investigate.[28] Uncertain about how to treat such cases, Pliny, the governor of Bythynia (a province in Asia Minor), wrote (c. 112) to Trajan, the emperor, requesting clarification:

> It is my custom, Lord Emperor, to refer to you all questions whereof I am in doubt. Who can better guide me . . . ? I have never participated in investigations of Christians; hence I do not know what is the crime usually punished or investigated, or what allowances are made . . . Meanwhile, this is the course I have taken with those who were accused before me as Christians. I asked them whether they were Christians, and I asked them a second and third time with threats of punishment. If they kept to it, I ordered them taken off for execution, for *I had no doubt that whatever it was they admitted, in any case they deserve to be punished for obstinacy and unbending pertinacity . . . As for those who said they neither were nor ever had been Christians, I thought it right to let them go*, when they recited a prayer to the gods at my dictation, and made supplication with incense and wine to your statue, which I had ordered to be brought into court for the purpose, and moreover, cursed Christ—things which (so it is said) those who are really Christians cannot be made to do.[29]

Trajan replied with approval for Pliny's handling of the matter:

> You have adopted the proper course, my dear Secundus, in your examination of the cases of those who were accused before you as Christians, for indeed, nothing can be laid down as a general rule involving something like a set form of procedure. *They are not to be sought out; but if they are accused and convicted, they must be punished*—but on the condition that whoever denies that he is a Christian, and makes the fact plain by his action, that is, by worshipping our gods, shall obtain pardon on his repentance, however suspicious his past conduct may be.[30]

But Trajan advised Pliny against accepting anonymous accusations, "since they are a bad example, and unworthy of our time." Pliny and Trajan agreed that anyone who would refuse such a gesture of loyalty must have serious crimes to hide, especially since the penalty for refusing was immediate execution.

Justin, a philosopher who had converted to Christianity (c. 150–155 A.D.), boldly wrote to the Emperor Antoninus Pius and to his son, the future emperor, Marcus Aurelius, whom he addressed as a colleague in philosophy and "a lover of learning,"[31] protesting the injustice Christians endured in imperial courts. Justin relates a recent case in Rome: a woman who had participated with her husband and their servants in various forms of sexual activity, fueled by wine, then converted to Christianity through the influence of her teacher Ptolemy, and subsequently refused to take part in such activities. Her friends persuaded her not to divorce, hoping for some reconciliation. But when she learned that, on a trip to Alexandria in Egypt, her husband had acted more flagrantly than ever, she sued for divorce and left him. Her outraged husband immediately brought a legal accusation against her, "affirming that she was a Christian." When she won a plea to delay her trial, her husband attacked her teacher in Christianity. Judge Urbicus, hearing the accusation, asked Ptolemy only one question: Was he a Christian? When he acknowledged that he was, Urbicus immediately sentenced him to death. Hearing this order, a man in the courtroom named Lucias challenged the judge:

> "What is the good of this judgment? Why have you punished this man, not as an adulterer, nor fornicator, nor thief, nor robber, nor convicted of any crime at all, but one who has only confessed that he is called by the name of Christian? This judgment of yours, Urbicus, does not become the Emperor Pius, nor the philosopher, the son of Caesar [Marcus Aurelius], nor the sacred Senate."[32]

Urbicus replied only, "You also seem to be one." And when Lucias said "Indeed I am," Urbicus condemned him—and a second protester in the audience—to follow Ptolemy to death.

Recounting this story, Justin points out that anyone can use the charge of Christianity to settle any personal grudge against a Christian: "I, too, therefore, expect to be plotted against and crucified"[33]—perhaps, he adds, by one of his professional rivals, the Cynic philosopher named Crescens. And Justin was right: apparently it was Crescens whose accusation led to his own arrest, trial, and condemnation in A.D. 165. Rusticus, a personal friend of Marcus Aurelius (who, by that time, had succeeded his father as emperor), conducted the trial. Rusticus ordered Justin's execution along with that of a whole group of his students, whose crime was learning Christian philosophy from him. The record of their trial shows that Rusticus asked Justin,

"Where do you meet?" . . . "Wherever it is each one's preference or opportunity," said Justin. "In any case, do you suppose we can all meet in the same place? Not so; for the Christians' God is not circumscribed by place; invisible, he fills the heavens and the earth, and is worshipped and glorified by believers everywhere."

Rusticus the prefect said, "Tell me, where do you meet? Where do you gather together your disciples?"

Justin said, "I have been living above the baths of a certain Martinus, son of Timiotinus, and for the entire period of my stay at Rome (and this is my second) I have known no other meeting place but there. Anyone who wished could come to my abode and I would impart to him the words of truth."

The prefect Rusticus said, "You do admit, then, that you are a Christian?" "Yes, I am," said Justin.[34]

Then Rusticus interrogated Cariton, the woman named Charito, Euelpistis, a slave in the imperial court, Hierax, Liberian, and Paeon—all of them Justin's students. All declared themselves Christians. The account proceeds:

"Well, then," said the prefect Rusticus, "let us come to the point at issue, a necessary and pressing business. Agree to offer sacrifice to the gods."

"No one of sound mind," said Justin, "turns from piety to impiety."

The prefect Rusticus said, "If you do not obey, you will be punished without mercy."[35]

When they replied, "Do what you will; we are Christians, and we do not offer sacrifice to idols," Rusticus pronounced sentence: "Let those who have refused to sacrifice to the gods and to yield to the emperor's edict be led away to be scourged and beheaded in accordance with the laws."[36]

Given this danger, what was a Christian to do? Once arrested and accused, should one confess to being a Christian, only to receive an order of execution: immediate beheading if one was fortunate enough to be a Roman citizen, like Justin and his companions, or, for noncitizens, extended torture as a spectacle in the public sports arena? Or should one deny it and make the token gesture of loyalty—intending afterwards to atone for the lie?

Charged with the unpleasant duty of ordering executions for noncompliance, Roman officials often tried to persuade the accused to save their own lives. According to contemporary accounts (c. 165), after the aged and revered Bishop Polycarp of Smyrna, in Asia Minor, was arrested by the police,

> the governor tried to persuade him to recant, saying, "Have respect for your age," *and other similar things that they usually say*; "Swear by the *genius* of the emperor. Recant. Say, 'Away with the atheists!' " Polycarp, with a sober expression, looked at all the mob of lawless pagans who were in the stadium . . . and said, "Away with the atheists!" The governor persisted and said, "Swear and I will let you go. Curse Christ!" But Polycarp answered, "For eighty-six years I have been his servant, and he has done me no wrong . . . If you delude yourself into thinking that I will swear by the emperor's *genius*, as you say, and if you pretend not to know who I am, listen and I will tell you plainly: I am a Christian."[37]

Polycarp was burned alive in the public arena.

An account from North Africa (c. 180) describes how the proconsul Saturninus, confronted by nine men and three women arraigned as Christians, worked to spare their lives, saying,

> "If you return to your senses, you can obtain pardon of our lord the emperor . . . We too are a religious people, and our religion is a simple one: We swear by the *genius* of our lord the emperor and offer prayers for his health—as you ought to do too."[38]

Meeting their determined resistance, Saturninus asked, "You wish no time for reconsideration?" Speratus, one of the accused, replied, "In so just a matter, there is no need for consideration." In spite of this, the proconsul ordered a thirty-day reprieve with the words "Think it over." But thirty days later, after interrogating the accused, Saturninus was forced to give the order:

> Whereas Speratus, Narzalus, Cittinus, Donata, Vestia, Secunda, and the others have confessed that they have been living in accordance with the rites of the Christians, and whereas, though they have been given the opportunity to return to the Roman usage, they have persevered in their obstinancy, they are hereby condemned to be executed by the sword.[39]

Speratus said, "We thank God!" Narzalus said, "Today we are martyrs in heaven. Thanks be to God!"

Such behavior provoked the scorn of the Stoic Emperor Marcus Aurelius, who despised the Christians as morbid and misguided exhibitionists. Many today might agree with his judgment, or else dismiss the martyrs as neurotic masochists. Yet for Jews and Christians of the first and second centuries, the term bore a different connotation: *martus* simply means, in Greek, "witness." In the Roman Empire, as in many countries throughout the world today, members of certain religious groups fell under government suspicion as organizations that fostered criminal or treasonous activities. Those who, like Justin, dared to protest publicly the unjust treatment Christians received in court made themselves likely targets of police action. For those caught in such a situation then, as now, the choice was often simple: either to speak out, risking arrest, torture, the formality of a futile trial, and exile or death—or to keep silent and remain safe. Their fellow believers revered those who spoke out as "confessors" and regarded only those who actually endured through death as "witnesses" (*martyres*).

But not all Christians spoke out. Many, at the moment of decision, made the opposite choice. Some considered martyrdom foolish, wasteful of human life, and so, contrary to God's will. They argued that "Christ, having died for us, was killed so that we might not be killed."[40] As past events become matters of religious conviction only when they serve to interpret present experience, here the interpretation of Christ's death became the focus for controversy over the practical question of martyrdom.

The orthodox who expressed the greatest concern to refute "heretical" gnostic views of Christ's passion were, without exception, persons who knew from firsthand experience the dangers to which Christians were exposed—and who insisted on the necessity of accepting martyrdom. When that great opponent of heresy, Ignatius, Bishop of Antioch, was arrested and tried, he is said to have accepted the death sentence with joyful exultation as his opportunity to "imitate the passion of my God!"[41] Condemned to be sent from Syria to Rome to be killed by wild beasts in the public amphitheater, Ignatius, chained and heavily guarded, wrote to the Christians in Rome, pleading with them not to interfere in his behalf:

> I am writing to all the churches, and I give injunction to everyone, that I am dying willingly for God's sake, if you do not prevent it. I plead with you not to be an "unseasonable kindness" to me. Allow me to be eaten by the beasts, through whom I can attain to God. I am God's wheat, and I am ground by the teeth of wild beasts, so that I may become pure bread of Christ . . . Do me this favor . . . Let there come upon me fire, and the cross, and struggle with wild beasts, cutting and tearing apart, racking of bones,

mangling of limbs, crushing of my whole body . . . may I
but attain to Jesus Christ![42]

What does Christ's passion mean to him? Ignatius says that
"Jesus Christ . . . was truly persecuted under Pontius Pilate, was
truly crucified, and died."[43] He vehemently opposes gnostic
Christians, whom he calls "atheists" for suggesting that since
Christ was a spiritual being, he only *appeared* to suffer and die:

> But if, as some say . . . his suffering was only an appear-
> ance, then *why am I a prisoner, and why do I long to fight
> with the wild beasts? In that case, I am dying in vain.*[44]

Ignatius complains that those who qualify his view of Christ's
suffering "are not moved by my own personal sufferings; for
they think the same things about me!"[45] His gnostic opponents,
challenging his understanding of Christ's passion, directly call
into question the value of his voluntary martyrdom.

Justin, whom tradition calls "the martyr," declares that
before his own conversion, when he was still a Platonist
philosopher, he personally witnessed Christians enduring public
torture and execution. Their courage, he says, convinced him
of their divine inspiration.[46] Protesting the world-wide persecution of Christians, he mentions those persecuted in Palestine
(c. 135):

> It is clear that no one can terrify or subdue us who
> believe in Jesus Christ, throughout the whole world. For it
> is clear that though beheaded, and crucified, and thrown to
> the wild beasts, in chains, in fire, and all other kinds of
> torture, we do not give up our confession; but the more
> such things happen, the more do others, in larger numbers,
> become believers.[47]

Consistent with his personal convictions concerning martyrdom
and his courageous acceptance of his own death sentence is
Justin's view that "Jesus Christ, our teacher, who was born for
this purpose, was crucified under Pontius Pilate and died, and

rose again."[48] Justin concludes his second *Apology* ("Defense" for the Christians) saying that he has written it for the sole purpose of refuting "wicked and deceitful" gnostic ideas. He attacks those who, he says, are "called Christians," but whom he considers heretics—followers of Simon, Marcion, and Valentinus.[49] "We do not know," he says darkly—combining admission with insinuation—whether they actually indulge in promiscuity or cannibalism, but, he adds, "we do know" one of their crimes: unlike the orthodox, "they are neither persecuted nor put to death" as martyrs.

Irenaeus, the great opponent of the Valentinians, was, like his predecessors, a man whose life was marked by persecution. He mentions many who were martyred in Rome, and he knew from personal experience the loss of his beloved teacher Polycarp, caught in mob violence, condemned, and burned alive among his enemies. Only twelve years later, in the summer of 177, Irenaeus witnessed growing hostility to Christians in his own city, Lyons. First they were prohibited from entering public places—the markets and the baths. Then, when the provincial governor was out of the city,

> the mob broke loose. Christians were hounded and attacked openly. They were treated as public enemies, assaulted, beaten, and stoned. Finally they were dragged into the Forum . . . were accused, and, after confessing to being Christians, they were flung in prison.[50]

An influential friend, Vettius Epagathus, who tried to intervene at their trial, was shouted down: "The prefect merely asked him if he too was a Christian. When he admitted, in the clearest voice, that he was,"[51] the prefect sentenced him to death along with the others. Their servants, tortured to extract information, finally "confessed" that, as the Romans suspected, their Christian employers committed sexual atrocities and cannibalism. An eyewitness account reports that this evidence turned the population against them: "These stories got around, and all the people raged against us, so that even those whose attitude had been moderate before because of their friendship with us now became greatly angry and gnashed their teeth against us."[52]

Every day new victims—the most outspoken members of the churches in Lyons or the neighboring town of Vienne, twenty miles down the Rhône River, were arrested and brutally tortured in prison as they awaited the day set for the mass execution, August 1. This was a holiday to celebrate the greatness of Rome and the emperor. Such occasions required the governor to display his patriotism by sponsoring lavish public entertainment for the whole population of the city. These obligations burdened provincial officials with enormous expenses for hiring professional gladiators, boxers, wrestling teams, and swordsmen. But the year before, the emperor and the Senate had passed a new law to offset the cost of gladitorial shows. Now the governor could legally substitute condemned criminals who were non-citizens, offering the spectacle of their torture and execution instead of athletic exhibitions—at the cost of six aurei per head, one-tenth the cost of hiring a fifth-class gladiator, with proportionate savings for the higher grades. This consideration no doubt added incentive to the official zeal against Christians, who could provide, as they did in Lyons, the least expensive holiday entertainment.

The story of one of the confessors in Lyons, the slave woman Blandina, illustrates what happened:

> All of us were in terror; and Blandina's earthly mistress, who was herself among the martyrs in the conflict, was in agony lest because of her bodily weakness she would not be able to make a bold confessor of her faith. Yet Blandina was filled with such power that even those who were taking turns to torture her in every way from dawn to dusk were weary and exhausted. They themselves admitted that they were beaten, that there was nothing further they could do to her, and they were surprised that she was still breathing, for her entire body was broken and torn.

On the day set for the gladitorial games, Blandina, along with three of her companions, Maturus, Sanctus, and Attalus, were led into the amphitheater:

> Blandina was hung on a post and exposed as bait for the wild animals that were let loose on her. She seemed to hang there in the form of a cross, and by her fervent prayer she aroused intense enthusiasm in those who were undergoing their ordeal . . . But none of the animals had touched her, and so she was taken down from the post and brought back to the jail to be preserved for another ordeal . . . tiny, weak, and insignificant as she was, she would give inspiration to her brothers . . . Finally, on the last day of the gladitorial games, they brought back Blandina again, this time with a boy of fifteen named Ponticus. Every day they had been brought in to watch the torture of the others, while attempts were made to force them to swear by the pagan idols. And because they persevered and condemned their persecutors, the crowd grew angry with them, so that . . . they subjected them to every atrocity and led them through every torture in turn.

After having run through the gauntlet of whips, having been mauled by animals, and forced into an iron seat placed over a fire to scorch his flesh, Ponticus died. Blandina, having survived the same tortures,

> was at last tossed into a net and exposed to a bull. After being tossed a good deal by the animal, she no longer perceived what was happening . . . Thus she too was offered in sacrifice, while the pagans themselves admitted that no woman had ever suffered so much in their experience.[53]

Although Irenaeus himself somehow managed to escape arrest, his association with those in prison compelled him to bring an account of their terrible suffering to Christians in Rome. When he returned to Gaul, he found the community in mourning: nearly fifty Christians had died in the two-month ordeal. He himself was persuaded to take over the leadership of the community, succeeding the ninety-year-old Bishop Pothinus, who had died of torture and exposure in prison.

In spite of all this, Irenaeus expresses no hostility against his fellow townsmen—but plenty against the gnostic "heretics." Like Justin, he attacks them as "false brethren" who

> have reached such a pitch of audacity that *they even pour contempt upon the martyrs, and vituperate those who are killed on account of confessing the Lord*, and *who . . . thereby strive to follow in the footsteps of the Lord's passion*, themselves bearing witness to the one who suffered.[54]

This declaration concludes his detailed attack on the Valentinian interpretation of Christ's passion. Condemning as blasphemy their claim that only Christ's *human* nature experiences suffering, while his divine nature transcends it, Irenaeus insists that

> *the same being who was seized and experienced suffering, and shed his blood for us, was both Christ and the Son of God* . . . and he became the Savior of those who would be delivered over to death for their confession of him, and lose their lives.[55]

Indeed, he adds, "if any one supposes that there were two natures in Christ," the one who suffered was certainly superior to the one who escaped suffering, sustaining neither injury nor insult." In the day of judgment, he warns, when the martyrs "attain to glory, then all who have cast a slur upon their martyrdom shall be confounded by Christ."[56]

Tertullian, another fierce opponent of heresy, describes how the sight of Christians tortured and dying initiated his own conversion: he saw a condemned Christian, dressed up by Roman guards to look like the god Attis, torn apart alive in the arena; another, dressed as Hercules, was burned alive. He admits that he, too, once enjoyed "the ludicrous cruelties of the noonday exhibition,"[57] watching another man, dressed as the god Mercury, testing the bodies of the tortured with a red-hot iron, and one dressed as Pluto, god of the dead, dragging corpses out of the arena. After his own conversion Tertullian, like Irenaeus, connected the teaching of Christ's passion and death with his own enthusiasm for martyrdom: "You must take up your cross and bear it after your Master . . . The sole key to unlock Paradise is your own life's blood."[58] Tertullian traces the rise of heresy directly to the outbreak of persecution. This, he says, impelled terrified believers to look for theological means to justify their cowardice:

> This among Christians is a time of persecution. *When, therefore, the faith is greatly agitated and the church on fire . . . then the gnostics break out; then the Valentinians creep forth; then all the opponents of martyrdom bubble up* . . . for they know that many Christians are simple and inexperienced and weak, and . . . they perceive that they will never be applauded more than when fear has opened the entries of the soul, especially when some terrorism has already arrayed with a crown the faith of martyrs.[59]

To what he considers "heretical" arguments against martyrdom Tertullian replies:

> Now we are in the midst of an intense heat, the very dogstar of persecution . . . the fire and the sword have tried some Christians, and the beasts have tried others; others are in prison, longing for martyrdoms which they have tasted already, having been beaten by clubs and tortured . . . We ourselves, having been appointed for pursuit, are like hares being hemmed in from a distance—*and the heretics go about as usual!*[60]

This situation, he explains, inspired him to attack as heretics those "who oppose martyrdom, representing salvation to be destruction," and who call encouragement to martyrdom foolish and cruel.

Hippolytus, the learned Greek teacher in Rome, also had witnessed the terror of the persecution under the Emperor Severus in the year 202. Hippolytus' zeal for martyrdom, like Tertullian's, was matched by his hatred of heresy. He concludes his massive *Refutation of All Heresies* insisting that only orthodox doctrine concerning Christ's incarnation and passion enables the believer to endure persecution:

> *If he were not of the same nature with ourselves, he would command in vain that we should imitate the teacher* . . . He did not protest against his passion, but became obedient unto death . . . now in all these acts *he offered up, as the first fruits, his own humanity, in order that you, when you are in tribulation, may not be discouraged, but, confessing yourself to be one like the redeemer,* may dwell in expectation of receiving what the Father has granted to the Son.[61]

In his mid-seventies, Hippolytus himself fulfilled his own exhortation: arrested on the order of the Emperor Maximin in 235, he was deported to Sardinia, where he died.

What pattern, then, do we observe? The opponents of heresy in the second century—Ignatius, Polycarp, Justin, Irenaeus, Tertullian, Hippolytus—are unanimous both in proclaiming Christ's passion and death and in affirming martyrdom. Also, they all accuse the heretics of false teaching about Christ's suffering and of "opposing martyrdom." Irenaeus declares:

> *The church in every place, because of the love which she cherishes toward God, sends forth, throughout all time, a multitude of martyrs to the Father; while all others not only have nothing of this kind to point to among themselves, but even maintain that bearing witness (martyrium) is not at all necessary* . . . with the exception, perhaps, of one or two among them . . . who have occasionally, along with our martyrs, borne the reproach of the name . . . For the church alone sustains with purity the reproach of those who suffer persecution for righteousness' sake, and endure all sorts of punishments, and are put to death because of the love which they bear toward God, and their confession of his Son.[62]

Irenaeus here denies to gnostics who die for the faith even the name of martyrs: at best they are only "a sort of retinue" granted to the *true* martyrs, who are orthodox Christians.

Although Irenaeus undoubtedly exaggerated the infrequency of martyrdom among the heretics, martyrdom did occur rarely among gnostic Christians. The reason was not simply cowardice, as the orthodox charged, but also the differences of opinion among them. What attitudes did gnostics take toward martyrdom, and on what grounds? Evidence from Nag Hammadi shows that their views were astonishingly diverse. Some advocated it; others repudiated it on principle. Followers of Valentinus took a mediating position between these extremes. But one thing is clear: in every case, the attitude toward martyrdom corresponds to the interpretation of Christ's suffering and death.

Some groups of gnostics, like the orthodox, insisted that Christ really suffered and died. It is claimed that several texts discovered at Nag Hammadi, including the *Secret Book of James*, the *Second Apocalypse of James*, and the *Apocalypse of Peter*, were written by disciples known to have undergone martyrdom —James, the brother of Jesus, and Peter. The author of the *Secret Book of James*, probably a Christian living in the second century who was anxious about the prospect of persecution, places himself in the situation of James and Peter. As they anticipate undergoing torture and death, he reports, they receive a vision of the risen Lord, who interprets the ordeals they face in terms of his own:

> . . . If you are oppressed by Satan and persecuted, and you do his [the Father's] will, I [say] that he will love you and make you equal with me . . . *Do you not know that you have yet to be abused and to be accused unjustly; and have yet to be shut up in prison, and condemned unlawfully, and crucified ⟨without⟩ reason, and buried ⟨shamefully⟩, as I (was) myself?* . . . Truly I say to you, none will be saved unless they believe in my cross. But those who have believed in my cross, theirs is the kingdom of God. . . . Truly I say to you, none of those who fear death will be saved; for *the kingdom of death belongs to those who put themselves to death.*[63]

This gnostic author not only insists that Christ really suffered and died, but even encourages believers to choose suffering and death. Like Ignatius, this gnostic teacher believes that one becomes identified with Christ through suffering: "Make yourselves like the Son of the Holy Spirit!"[64]

The same concern with persecution, and a similar analogy between the believer's experience and the Savior's passion, dominates the *Second Apocalypse of James*. The Savior, "who lived [without] blasphemy, died by means of [blasphemy]."[65] As he dies he says, "I am surely dying, but I shall be found in life."[66] The *Apocalypse* climaxes with the brutal scene of James's own torture and death by stoning:

> . . . the priests . . . found him standing beside the columns of the temple, beside the mighty corner stone. And they decided to throw him down from the height, and they cast him down. And . . . they seized him and [struck] him as they dragged him on the ground. They stretched him out, and placed a stone on his abdomen. They all placed their feet on him, saying, "You have erred!" Again they raised him up, since he was alive, and made him dig a hole. They made him stand in it. After having covered him up to his abdomen, they stoned him.[67]

As he dies he offers a prayer intended to strengthen other Christians who face martyrdom. Like Jesus, James is "surely dying," but "shall be found in life."

But while some gnostics affirmed the reality of Christ's passion and expressed enthusiasm for martyrdom, others denied that reality and attacked such enthusiasm. The *Testimony of Truth* declares that enthusiasts for martyrdom do not know "who Christ is":

> The foolish—thinking in their heart that if they confess, "We are Christians," in word only [but] not with power, while giving themselves over to ignorance, to a human death, not knowing where they are going, nor who Christ is, thinking that they will live, when they are (really) in

error—hasten toward the principalities and authorities. They fall into their clutches because of the ignorance that is in them.[68]

The author ridicules the popular view that martyrdom ensures salvation: if it were that simple, he says, *everyone* would confess Christ and be saved! Those who live under such illusions

> are [empty] martyrs, since they bear witness only [to] themselves. . . . When they are "perfected" with a (martyr's) death, this is what they are thinking: "If we deliver ourselves over to death for the sake of the Name, we shall be saved." These matters are not settled in this way. . . . They do not have the Word which gives [life].[69]

This gnostic author attacks specific views of martyrdom familiar from orthodox sources. First, he attacks the conviction that the martyr's death offers forgiveness of sins, a view expressed, for example, in the orthodox account of Polycarp's martyrdom: "Through suffering of one hour they purchase for themselves eternal life."[70] Tertullian, too, declares that he himself desires to suffer "that he may obtain from God complete forgiveness, by giving in exchange his blood."[71] Second, this author ridicules orthodox teachers who, like Ignatius and Tertullian, see martyrdom as an offering to God and who have the idea that God desires "human sacrifice": such a belief makes God into a cannibal. Third, he attacks those who believe that martyrdom ensures their resurrection. Rusticus, the Roman judge, asked Justin, only moments before ordering his execution, "Listen, you who are considered educated . . . do you suppose you will ascend to heaven?" Justin answered, "I do not *suppose* it, but I know it certainly and am fully persuaded of it."[72] But the *Testimony of Truth* declares that such Christians are only "destroying themselves"—they were deluded into thinking that Christ shared their own mortality, when in reality he, being filled with divine power, was alien to suffering and to death:

> The Son of Man [came] forth from imperishability, [being] alien to defilement. . . . he went down to Hades

and performed mighty works. He raised the dead therein
. . . and he also destroyed their works from among men, so
that the lame, the blind, the paralytic, and the dumb, (and)
the demon-possessed were granted healing. . . . For this
reason he [destroyed] his flesh from [the cross] which he
[bore].[73]

The *Apocalypse of Peter* discloses how Peter, noted for his
misunderstanding, becomes enlightened and discovers the true
secret of Jesus' passion. The author of this book, like the author
of the *Secret Book of James*, apparently was a gnostic Christian
concerned with the threat of persecution. As the *Apocalypse*
opens, "Peter" fears that he and his Lord face the same danger:
". . . I saw the priests and the people running up to us with
stones as if they would kill us; and I was afraid we were going
to die."[74] But Peter falls into an ecstatic trance and receives a
vision of the Lord, who warns him that many who "accept our
teaching in the beginning"[75] will fall into error. These "false
believers" (described, of course, from the gnostic viewpoint)
represent orthodox Christians. All who fall under their influence
"shall become their prisoners, since they are without perception."[76]

What the gnostic author dislikes most about these Christians
is that they coerce innocent fellow believers "to the executioner"
—apparently the forces of the Roman state—under the illusion
that if they "hold fast to the name of a dead man," confessing
the crucified Christ, "they will become pure."[77] The author says,

". . . These are the ones who oppress their brothers,
saying to them, 'Through this [martyrdom] our God shows
mercy, since salvation comes to us from this.' They do not
know the punishment of those who are gladdened by those
who have done this deed to the little ones who have been
sought out and imprisoned."[78]

The author rejects orthodox propaganda for martyrdom—that
it earns salvation—and expresses horror at their exclamations of
joy over acts of violence done to the "little ones." In this way

the catholic community will "set forth a harsh fate";[79] many believers "will be ground to pieces among them."[80]

Yet while the *Apocalypse of Peter* rejects the orthodox view of martyrdom, it does not reject martyrdom altogether: "others of those who suffer" (that is, those who have attained *gnosis*) acquire a new understanding of the meaning of their own suffering; they understand that it "will perfect the wisdom of the brotherhood that really exists."[81] In place of the teaching that enslaves believers—the orthodox teaching of the crucified Christ—the Savior gives Peter the new vision of his passion that we noted before:

> . . . He whom you saw being glad and laughing above the cross, he is the Living Jesus. But he into whose hands and feet they are driving the nails is his fleshly part, which is the substitute. They put to shame that which remained in his likeness. And look at him, and (look at) me!"[82]

Through this vision, Peter learns to face suffering. Initially, he feared that he and the Lord "would die"; now he understands that only the body, "the fleshly counterpart," the "substitute," can die. The Lord explains that the "primal part," the intelligent spirit, is released to join "the perfect light with my holy spirit."[83]

Gnostic sources written by Valentinus and his followers are more complex than either those which simply affirm Christ's passion or those which claim that, apart from his mortal body, Christ remained utterly impervious to suffering. Several major Valentinian texts discovered at Nag Hammadi clearly acknowledge Jesus' passion and death. The *Gospel of Truth*, which Quispel attributes to Valentinus or a follower of his, tells how Jesus, "nailed to a tree," was "slain."[84] Extending the common Christian metaphor, the author envisions Jesus on the cross as fruit on a tree, a new "fruit of the tree of knowledge" that yields life, not death:

> . . . nailed to a tree; he became a fruit of the knowledge [*gnosis*] of the Father, which did not, however, become destructive because it ⟨was⟩ eaten, but gave to those who

ate it cause to become glad in the discovery. For he discovered them in himself, and they discovered him in themselves . . .[85]

Contrary to orthodox sources, which interpret Christ's death as a sacrifice redeeming humanity from guilt and sin, this gnostic gospel sees the crucifixion as the occasion for discovering the divine self within. Yet with this different interpretation, the *Gospel of Truth* gives a moving account of Jesus' death:

> . . . the merciful one, the faithful one, Jesus, was patient in accepting sufferings . . . since he knows that his death is life for many. . . . He was nailed to a tree . . . He draws himself down to death though eternal life clothes him. Having stripped himself of the perishable rags, he put on imperishability . . .[86]

Another remarkable Valentinian text, the *Tripartite Tractate*, introduces the Savior as "the one who will be begotten and who will suffer."[87] Moved by compassion for humanity, he willingly became

> what they were. So, for their sake, he became manifest in an involuntary suffering. . . . Not only did he take upon himself the death of those whom he intended to save, but also he accepted their smallness . . . He let himself be conceived and born as an infant in body and soul.[88]

Yet the Savior's nature is a paradox. The *Tripartite Tractate* explains that the one who is born and who suffers is the Savior foreseen by the Hebrew prophets; what they did not envision is "that which he was before, and what he is eternally, an unbegotten, impassible Word, who came into being in flesh."[89] Similarly, the *Gospel of Truth*, having described Jesus' human death, goes on to say that

> the Word of the Father goes forth into the all . . . purifying it, bringing it back into the Father, into the Mother, Jesus of the infiniteness of gentleness.[90]

A third Valentinian text, the *Interpretation of the Gnosis*, articulates the same paradox. On the one hand the Savior becomes vulnerable to suffering and death; on the other, he is the Word, full of divine power. The Savior explains: "I became very small, so that through my humility I might take you up to the great height, whence you had fallen."[91]

None of these sources denies that Jesus actually suffered and died; all assume it. Yet all are concerned to show how, in his incarnation, Christ transcended human nature so that he could prevail over death by divine power.[92] The Valentinians thereby initiate discussion of the problem that became central to Christian theology some two hundred years later—the question of how Christ could be simultaneously human and divine. For this, Adolf von Harnack, historian of Christianity, calls them the "first Christian theologians."

What does this mean for the question of martyrdom? Irenaeus accuses the Valentinians of "pouring contempt" on the martyrs and "casting a slur upon their martyrdom." What is their position? Heracleon, the distinguished gnostic teacher, himself a student of Valentinus', directly discusses martyrdom as he comments on Jesus' saying:

> ". . . every one who acknowledges me before men, the Son of Man also will acknowledge before the angels of God; but he who denies me before men will be denied before the angels of God. . . . And when they bring you before . . . the rulers and the authorities, do not be anxious how or what you are to answer . . ."[93]

Heracleon considers the question, What does it mean to "confess Christ"? He explains that people confess Christ in different ways. Some confess Christ in their faith and in their everyday conduct. However, most people consider only the second type of confession—making a verbal confession ("I am a Christian") before a magistrate. The latter, he says, is what "the many" (orthodox Christians) consider to be the *only* confession. But, Heracleon points out, "even hypocrites can make this confession." What is required universally of all Christians, he says, is the first type of confession; the second is required of some, but not of all. Disciples like Matthew, Philip, and Thomas never "confessed" before the magistrates; still, he declares, they confessed Christ in the superior way, "in faith and conduct throughout their whole lives."[94]

In naming these specific disciples, who often typify gnostic initiates (as in the *Gospel of Philip* and the *Gospel of Thomas*), Heracleon implies that they are superior to such martyr-apostles as Peter, whom the Valentinians consider typical of "the many" —that is, of merely *orthodox* Christians. Is he saying that martyrdom is fine for ordinary Christians, but not necessary for gnostics? Is he offering a rationale for gnostics to avoid martyrdom?

If that is what he means, he avoids stating it directly: his comments remain ambiguous. For he goes on to say that although confessing Christ "in faith and conduct" is more universal, this leads naturally to making an open confession at a trial, "if necessity and reason dictate." What makes such confession "necessary" and "rational"? Simply that a Christian accused before a judge cannot *deny* Christ: in that case, Heracleon admits, verbal confession is the necessary and rational alternative to denial.

Yet Heracleon articulates a wholly different attitude toward martyrdom from his orthodox contemporaries. He expresses none of their enthusiasm for martyrdom, none of their praise for the "glorious victory" earned through death. Above all, he never suggests that the believers' suffering imitates Christ's. For if only the *human* element in Christ experienced the passion, this suggests that the believer, too, suffers only on a human level while the divine spirit within transcends suffering and death. Apparently the Valentinians considered the martyr's "blood witness" to be second best to the superior, *gnostic* witness to Christ—a view that could well have provoked Irenaeus' anger that these gnostics "show contempt" for the martyrs and devalue what he considers the "ultimate sacrifice."

Although Irenaeus acknowledges that the gnostics are attempting to raise the level of theological understanding, he declares that "they cannot accomplish a reformation effective enough to compensate for the harm they are doing."[95] From his viewpoint, any argument that Christians could use to avoid martyrdom undermines the solidarity of the whole Christian community. Rather than identifying with those held in prison, facing torture or execution, gnostic Christians might withdraw support from those they consider overzealous and unenlightened fanatics. Such actions serve, Irenaeus says, to "cut in pieces the great and glorious body of Christ [the church] and . . . destroy it."[96] Preserving unity demands that all Christians confess Christ "persecuted under Pontius Pilate, crucified, dead, and buried," implicitly affirming the necessity of the "blood witness" that imitates his passion.

Why did the orthodox view of martyrdom—and of Christ's death as its model—prevail? I suggest that persecution gave impetus to the formation of the organized church structure that developed by the end of the second century. To place the question in a contemporary context, consider what recourse remains to dissidents facing a massive and powerful political system: they attempt to publicize cases of violence and injustice to arouse world-wide public support. The torture and execution of a small group of persons known only to their relatives and friends soon fall into oblivion, but the cases of dissidents who are scientists, writers, Jews, or Christian missionaries may arouse the concern of an international community of those who identify with the victims by professional or religious affiliation.

There is, of course, a major difference between ancient and modern tactics. Today the purpose of such publicity is to generate pressure and gain the release of those who are tortured or imprisoned. The apologists, like Justin, did address the Roman authorities, protesting the unjust treatment of Christians and calling on them to end it. But Christians wrote the stories of the martyrs for a different purpose, and for a different audience. They wrote exclusively to other Christian churches, not in hope of ending persecution, but to warn them of their common danger, to encourage them to emulate the martyrs' "glorious victory," and to consolidate the communities internally and in relation to one another. So, in the second and third centuries, when Roman violence menaced Christian groups in remote provinces of the Empire, these events were communicated to Christians throughout the known world. Ignatius, condemned to execution in the Roman arena, occupied himself on his final journey writing letters to many provincial churches, telling them of his own situation and urging them to support the catholic ("universal") church organized around the bishops. He warned them above all to avoid heretics who deviate from the bishops' authority and from the orthodox doctrines of Christ's passion, death, and resurrection. His letters to the Christians in Rome, whom he had never met, testify to the efficacy of such communication: Ignatius was confident that they would intervene to prevent his execution if he allowed them to do so. Later, when some fifty Christians in Lyons and Vienne were arrested in June 177, they immediately wrote to "our brothers in Asia and Phyrgia who have the same faith," describing their suffering, and sent Irenaeus to inform the well-established church in Rome.

Pressed by their common danger, members of scattered Christian groups throughout the world increasingly exchanged letters and traveled from one church to another. Accounts of the martyrs, often taken from records of their trials and from eyewitnesses, circulated among the churches in Asia, Africa, Rome, Greece, Gaul, and Egypt. By such communication, members of the diversified earlier churches became aware of regional differences as obstacles to their claim to participate in one catholic church. As noted earlier, Irenaeus insisted that all churches throughout the world must agree on all vital points of doctrine, but even he was shocked when Victor, Bishop of Rome, attempted to move the regional churches toward greater uniformity. In 190, Victor demanded that Christians in Asia Minor abandon their traditional practice of celebrating Easter on Passover, and conform instead to Roman custom—or else give up their claim to be "catholic Christians." At the same time, the Roman church was compiling the definitive list of books eventually accepted by all Christian churches. Increasingly stratified orders of institutional hierarchy consolidated the communities internally and regularized communication with what Irenaeus called "the catholic church dispersed throughout the whole world, even to the ends of the earth"—a network of groups becoming increasingly uniform in doctrine, ritual, canon, and political structure.

Among outsiders, reports of brutality toward Christians aroused mixed emotions. Even the arrogant Tacitus, describing how Nero had Christians mocked and tortured to death, is moved to add:

> Even for criminals who deserve extreme and exemplary punishment, there arose a feeling of compassion; for it was not, as it seemed, for the public good, but to glut one man's cruelty, that they were being destroyed.[97]

Among the townspeople of Lyons, after the slaughter in the arena, some wanted to mutilate the corpses; others ridiculed the martyrs as fools, while others, "seeming to extend a measure of compassion," pondered what inspired their courage: "What advantage has their religion brought them, which they preferred to their own life?"[98] No doubt the persecutions terrified many into avoiding contact with Christians, but Justin and Tertullian both say that the sight of martyrs aroused the wonder and admiration that impelled them to investigate the movement, and then to join it. And both attest that this happened to many others. (As Justin remarked: "The more such things happen, the more do others, in larger numbers, become believers.")[99] Tertullian writes in defiance to Scapula, the proconsul of Carthage:

> Your cruelty is our glory . . . All who witness the noble patience of [the martyrs], are struck with misgivings, are inflamed with desire to examine the situation . . . and as soon as they come to know the truth, they immediately enroll themselves as its disciples.[100]

He boasts to the Roman prosecutor that "the oftener we are mown down by you, the more we grow in numbers: the blood of the Christians is seed!"[101] Those who followed the orthodox consensus in doctrine and church politics also belonged to the church that—confessing the crucified Christ—became conspicuous for its martyrs. Groups of gnostic Christians, on the other hand, were scattered and lost—those who resisted doctrinal conformity, questioned the value of the "blood witness," and often opposed submission to episcopal authority.

Finally, in its portrait of Christ's life and his passion, orthodox teaching offered a means of interpreting fundamental elements of human experience. Rejecting the gnostic view that Jesus was a spiritual being, the orthodox insisted that he, like the rest of humanity, was born, lived in a family, became hungry and tired, ate and drank wine, suffered and died. They even went so far as to insist that he rose *bodily* from the dead. Here again, as we have seen, orthodox tradition implicitly affirms bodily experience as the central fact of human life. What one does physically—one eats and drinks, engages in sexual life or avoids it, saves one's life or gives it up—all are vital elements in one's *religious* development. But those gnostics who regarded the essential part of every person as the "inner spirit" dismissed such physical experience, pleasurable or painful, as a distraction from spiritual reality—indeed, as an illusion. No wonder, then, that far more people identified with the orthodox portrait than with the "bodiless spirit" of gnostic tradition. Not only the martyrs, but all Christians who have suffered for 2,000 years, who have feared and faced death, have found their experience validated in the story of the *human* Jesus.

CHAPTER

V

Whose Church Is the "True Church"?

OR NEARLY 2,000 years, Christian tradition has preserved and revered orthodox writings that denounce the gnostics, while suppressing—and virtually destroying—the gnostic writings themselves. Now, for the first time, certain texts discovered at Nag Hammadi reveal the other side of the coin: how gnostics denounced the orthodox.[1] The *Second Treatise of the Great Seth* polemicizes against orthodox Christianity, contrasting it with the "true church" of the gnostics. Speaking for those he calls the sons of light, the author says:

> . . . we were hated and persecuted, not only by those who are ignorant [pagans], but also by those who think they are advancing the name of Christ, since they were unknowingly empty, not knowing who they are, like dumb animals.[2]

The Savior explains that such persons made an imitation of the true church, "having proclaimed a doctrine of a dead man and lies, so as to resemble the freedom and purity of the perfect church (*ekklesia*)."[3] Such teaching, he charges, reconciles its adherents to fear and slavery, encouraging them to subject themselves to the earthly representatives of the world creator, who, in his "empty glory," declares, "I am God, and there is no other beside me."[4] Such persons persecute those who have achieved liberation through *gnosis*, attempting to lead them astray from "the truth of their freedom."[5]

The *Apocalypse of Peter* describes, as noted before, catholic Christians as those who have fallen "into an erroneous name and into the hand of an evil, cunning man, with a teaching in a multiplicity of forms,"[6] allowing themselves to be ruled heretically. For, the author adds, they

> blaspheme the truth and proclaim evil teaching. And they
> will say evil things against each other. . . . many others . . .
> who oppose the truth and are the messengers of error . . .
> set up their error . . . against these pure thoughts of mine . . .[7]

The author takes each of the characteristics of the catholic church as evidence that this is only an imitation church, a counterfeit, a "sisterhood" that mimics the true Christian brotherhood. Such Christians, in their blind arrogance, claim exclusive legitimacy: "Some who do not understand mystery speak of things which they do not understand, but they will boast that the mystery of the truth belongs to them alone."[8] Their obedience to bishops and deacons indicates that they "bow to the judgment of the leaders."[9] They oppress their brethren, and slander those who attain *gnosis*.

The *Testimony of Truth* attacks ecclesiastical Christians as those who say "we are Christians," but "who [do not know who] Christ is."[10] But this same author goes on to attack other gnostics as well, including the followers of Valentinus, Basilides, and Simon, as brethren who are still immature. Another of the Nag Hammadi texts, the *Authoritative Teaching*, intends to demolish all teaching, especially orthodox teaching, that the author considers *un*authoritative. Like Irenaeus—but diametrically opposed —he says of "those who contend with us, being adversaries,"[11] that they are "dealers in bodies,"[12] senseless, ignorant, worse than pagans, because they have no excuse for their error.

The bitterness of these attacks on the "imitation church" probably indicates a late stage of the controversy. By the year 200, the battle lines had been drawn: both orthodox and gnostic Christians claimed to represent the true church and accused one another of being outsiders, false brethren, and hypocrites.

How was a believer to tell true Christians from false ones? Orthodox and gnostic Christians offered different answers, as each group attempted to define the church in ways that excluded the other. Gnostic Christians, claiming to represent only "the few," pointed to qualitative criteria. In protest against the majority, they insisted that baptism did not make a Christian: according to the *Gospel of Philip*, many people "go down into the water and come up without having received anything,"[13] and still they claimed to be Christians. Nor did profession of the creed, or even martyrdom, count as evidence: "anyone can do these things." Above all, they refused to identify the church with the actual, visible community that, they warned, often only imitated it. Instead, quoting a saying of Jesus ("By their fruits you shall know them") they required evidence of spiritual maturity to demonstrate that a person belonged to the true church.

But orthodox Christians, by the late second century, had begun to establish objective criteria for church membership. Whoever confessed the creed, accepted the ritual of baptism, participated in worship, and obeyed the clergy was accepted as a fellow Christian. Seeking to unify the diverse churches scattered throughout the world into a single network, the bishops eliminated qualitative criteria for church membership. Evaluating each candidate on the basis of spiritual maturity, insight, or personal holiness, as the gnostics did, would require a far more complex administration. Further, it would tend to exclude many who much needed what the church could give. To become truly *catholic*—universal—the church rejected all forms of elitism, attempting to include as many as possible within its embrace. In the process, its leaders created a clear and simple framework, consisting of doctrine, ritual, and political structure, that has proven to be an amazingly effective system of organization.

So the orthodox Ignatius, Bishop of Antioch, defines the church in terms of the bishop, who represents that system:

> Let no one do anything pertaining to the church without the bishop. Let that be considered a valid eucharist which is celebrated by the bishop, or by the person whom he appoints ... Wherever the bishop offers [the eucharist], let the congregation be present, just as, wherever Jesus Christ is, there is the catholic church.[14]

Lest any "heretic" suggest that Christ may be present even when the bishop is absent, Ignatius sets him straight:

> It is not legitimate either to baptize or to hold an *agapē* [cult meal] without the bishop ... To join with the bishop is to join the church; to separate oneself from the bishop is to separate oneself not only from the church, but from God himself.[15]

Apart from the church hierarchy, he insists, "there is nothing that can be called a church."[16]

Irenaeus, Bishop of Lyons, agrees with Ignatius that the only true church is that which "preserves the same form of ecclesiastical constitution":

> True *gnosis* is that which consists in the doctrine of the apostles, and the ancient constitution [*systema*] of the church throughout the whole world, and the character of the body of Christ according to the successions of bishops, by which they have handed down that which exists everywhere.[17]

Only this system, Irenaeus says, stands upon the "pillar and ground" of those apostolic writings to which he attributes absolute authority—above all, the gospels of the New Testament. All others are false and unreliable, unapostolic, and probably composed by heretics. The catholic church alone offers a "very complete system of doctrine,"[18] proclaiming, as we have seen, one God, creator and father of Christ, who became incarnate, suffered, died, and rose bodily from the dead. Outside of this church there is no salvation: "she is the entrance to life; all others are thieves and robbers."[19] As spokesman for the church of God, Irenaeus insists that those he calls heretics stand outside the church. All who reject his version of Christian truth are "false persons, evil seducers, and hypocrites" who "speak to the multitude about those in the church, whom they call *catholic*, or *ecclesiastical*."[20] Irenaeus says he longs to "convert them to the church of God"[21]—since he considers them apostates, worse than pagans.

Gnostic Christians, on the contrary, assert that what distinguishes the false from the true church is not its relationship to the clergy, but the level of understanding of its members, and the quality of their relationship with one another. The *Apocalypse of Peter* declares that "those who are from the life . . . having been enlightened,"[22] discriminate for themselves between what is true and false. Belonging to "the remnant . . . summoned to knowledge [*gnosis*],"[23] they neither attempt to dominate others nor do they subject themselves to the bishops and deacons, those "waterless canals." Instead they participate in "the wisdom of the brotherhood that really exists . . . the spiritual fellowship with those united in communion."[24]

The *Second Treatise of the Great Seth* similarly declares that what characterizes the true church is the union its members enjoy with God and with one another, "united in the friendship of friends forever, who neither know any hostility, nor evil, but who are united by my *gnosis* . . . (in) friendship with one another."[25] Theirs is the intimacy of marriage, a "spiritual wedding," since they live "in fatherhood and motherhood and rational brotherhood and wisdom"[26] as those who love each other as "fellow spirits."[27]

Such ethereal visions of the "heavenly church" contrast sharply with the down-to-earth portrait of the church that orthodox sources offer. Why do gnostic authors abandon concreteness and describe the church in fantastic and imaginative terms? Some scholars say that this proves that they understood little, and cared less, about social relationships. Carl Andresen, in his recent, massive study of the early Christian church, calls them "religious solipsists" who concerned themselves only with their own individual spiritual development, indifferent to the community responsibilities of a church.[28] But the sources cited above show that these gnostics defined the church *precisely* in terms of the quality of interrelationships among its members.

Orthodox writers described the church in concrete terms because they accept the status quo; that is, they affirmed that the actual community of those gathered for worship *was* "the church." Gnostic Christians dissented. Confronted with those in the churches whom they considered ignorant, arrogant, or self-interested, they refused to agree that the whole community of believers, without further qualification, constituted "the church." Dividing from the majority over such issues as the value of martyrdom, they intended to discriminate between the mass of believers and those who truly had *gnosis*, between what they called the imitation, or the counterfeit, and the true church.

Consider, for example, how specific disputes with other Christians drove even Hippolytus and Tertullian, those two fervent opponents of heresy, to redefine the church for themselves. Hippolytus shared his teacher Irenaeus' view of the church as the sole bearer of truth. Like Irenaeus, Hippolytus defined that truth as what the apostolic succession of bishops guaranteed on the basis of the canon and church doctrine. But when a deacon named Callistus was elected bishop of his church in Rome, Hippolytus protested vehemently. He publicized a scandalous story, slandering Callistus' integrity:

> Callistus was a slave of Carpophorus, a Christian employed in the imperial palace. To Callistus, as being of the faith, Carpophorus entrusted no inconsiderable amount of money, and directed him to bring in profit from banking. He took the money and started business in what is called Fish Market Ward. As time passed, not a few deposits were

entrusted to him by widows and brethren . . . Callistus, however, embezzled the lot, and became financially embarrassed.[29]

When Carpophorus heard of this, he demanded an accounting, but, Hippolytus says, Callistus absconded and fled: "finding a vessel in the port ready for a voyage, he went on board, intending to sail wherever she happened to be bound for."[30] When his master pursued him onto the ship, Callistus knew he was trapped, and, in desperation, jumped overboard. Rescued against his will by the sailors as the crowd on the shore shouted encouragement, Callistus was handed over to Carpophorus, returned to Rome, and placed in penal servitude. Apparently Hippolytus was trying to explain how Callistus came to be tortured and imprisoned, since many revered him as a martyr; Hippolytus maintained instead that he was a criminal. Hippolytus also objected to Callistus' views on the Trinity, and found Callistus' policy of extending forgiveness of sins to cover sexual transgressions shockingly "lax." And he denounced Callistus, the former slave, for allowing believers to regularize liaisons with their own slaves by recognizing them as valid marriages.

But Hippolytus found himself in the minority. The majority of Roman Christians respected Callistus as a teacher and martyr, endorsed his policies, and elected him bishop. Now that Callistus headed the Roman church, Hippolytus decided to break away from it. In the process, he turned against the bishop the same polemical techniques that Irenaeus had taught him to use against the gnostics. As Irenaeus singled out certain groups of Christians as heretics, and named them according to their teachers (as "Valentinians," "Simonians," etc.), so Hippolytus accused Callistus of teaching heresy and characterized his following as "the Callistians"—as if they were a sect separate from "the church," which Hippolytus himself claimed to represent.

How could Hippolytus justify his claim to represent the church, when he and his few adherents were attacking the great majority of Roman Christians and their bishop? Hippolytus explained that the majority of "self-professed Christians" were incapable of living up to the standard of the *true* church, which consisted of "the community of those who live in holiness." Like his gnostic opponents, having refused to identify the church through its official hierarchy, he characterized it instead in terms of the spiritual qualities of its members.

Tertullian presented an even more dramatic case. As long as he identified himself as a "catholic Christian," Tertullian defined the church as Irenaeus had. Writing his *Preemptive Objection against Heretics*, Tertullian proclaimed that his church alone bore the apostolic rule of faith, revered the canon of Scriptures, and bore through its ecclesiastical hierarchy the sanction of apostolic succession. Like Irenaeus, Tertullian indicted the heretics for violating each of these boundaries. He complains that they refused simply to accept and believe the rule of faith as others did: instead, they challenged others to raise theological questions, when they themselves claimed no answers,

> being ready to say, and sincerely, of certain points of their belief, "This is not so," and "I take this in a different sense," and "I do not admit that."[31]

Tertullian warns that such questioning leads to heresy: "This rule . . . was taught by Christ, and raises among ourselves no other questions than those which the heresies introduce and which make men heretics!"[32] He also charges that the heretics did not restrict themselves to the Scriptures of the New Testament: either they added other writings or they challenged the orthodox interpretation of key texts.[33] Further, as noted already, he condemns the heretics for being "a camp of rebels" who refused to submit to the authority of the bishop. Arguing for a strict order of obedience and submission, he concludes that "evidence of a stricter discipline existing among us is an additional proof of truth."[34]

So speaks Tertullian the catholic. But at the end of his life, when his own intense fervor impelled him to break with the orthodox community, he rejected and branded it as the church of mere "psychic" Christians. He joined instead the Montanist movement, whose adherents called it the "new prophecy," claiming to be inspired by the Holy Spirit. At this time Tertullian began to distinguish sharply between the empirical church and another, spiritual vision of the church. Now he no longer identified the church in terms of its ecclesiastical organization, but only with the spirit that sanctified individual members. He scorns the catholic community as "the church of a number of bishops":

> For the church itself, properly and principally, is spirit, in which there is the trinity of one divinity, Father, Son, and Holy Spirit. . . . The church congregates where the Lord plans it—a spiritual church for spiritual people—*not* the church of a number of bishops![35]

What impelled dissidents from catholic Christianity to maintain or develop such visionary descriptions of the church? Were their visions "up in the air" because they were interested in theoretical speculation? On the contrary, their motives were sometimes traditional and polemical, but also sometimes political. They were convinced that the "visible church"—the actual network of catholic communities—either had been wrong from the beginning or had gone wrong. The true church, by contrast, was "invisible": only its members perceived who belonged to it and who did not. Dissidents intended their idea of an invisible church to oppose the claims of those who said they represented the universal church. Martin Luther made the same move 1,300 years later. When his devotion to the Catholic Church changed to criticism, then rejection, he began to insist, with other protestant reformers, that the true church was "invisible"—that is, not identical with Catholicism.

The gnostic author of the *Testimony of Truth* would have agreed with Luther and gone much further. He rejects as fallacious all the marks of ecclesiastical Christianity. Obedience to the clerical hierarchy requires believers to submit themselves to "blind guides" whose authority comes from the malevolent creator. Conformity to the rule of faith attempts to limit all Christians to an inferior ideology: "They say, '[Even if] an [angel] comes from heaven, and preaches to you beyond what we preach to you, let him be accursed!' "[36] Faith in the sacraments shows naïve and magical thinking: catholic Christians practice baptism as an initiation rite which guarantees them "a hope of salvation,"[37] believing that only those who receive baptism are "headed for life."[38]

Against such "lies" the gnostic declares that "this, therefore, is the *true* testimony: when man knows himself, and God who is over the truth, he will be saved."[39] Only those who come to recognize that they have been living in ignorance, and learn to release themselves by discovering who they are, experience enlightenment as a new life, as "the resurrection." Physical rituals like baptism become irrelevant, for "the baptism of truth is something else; it is by renunciation of [the] world that it is found."[40]

Against those who claimed exclusive access to truth, those who followed law and authority, and who placed their faith in ritual, this author sets his own vision: "Whoever is able to renounce them [money and sexual intercourse] shows [that] he is [from] the generation of the [Son of Man], and that he has power to accuse [them]."[41] Like Hippolytus and Tertullian, but more radical than either, this teacher praises sexual abstinence and economic renunciation as the marks of the true Christian.

The *Authoritative Teaching*, another text discovered at Nag Hammadi, also offers vehement attack on catholic Christianity. The author tells the story of the soul, who originally came from heaven, from the "fullness of being,"[42] but when she "was cast into the body"[43] she experienced sensual desire, passions, hatred, and envy. Clearly the allegory refers to the individual soul's struggle against passions and sin; yet the language of the account suggests a wider, social referent as well. It relates the struggle of those who are spiritual, akin to the soul (with whom the author identifies), against those who are essentially alien to her. The author explains that some who were called "our brothers," who claimed to be Christians, actually were outsiders. Although "the word has been preached"[44] to them, and they heard "the call"[45] and performed acts of worship, these self-professed Christians were "worse than . . . the pagans,"[46] who had an excuse for their ignorance.

On what counts does the gnostic accuse these believers? First, that they "do not seek after God."[47] The gnostic understands Christ's message not as offering a set of answers, but as encouragement to engage in a process of searching: "seek and inquire about the ways you should go, since there is nothing else as good as this."[48] The rational soul longs to

> see with her mind, and perceive her kinsmen, and learn about her root . . . in order that she might receive what is hers . . .[49]

What is the result? The author declares that she attains fulfillment:

> . . . the rational soul who wearied herself in seeking— she learned about God. She labored with inquiring, enduring distress in the body, wearing out her feet after the evangelists, learning about the Inscrutable One. . . . She came to rest in him who is at rest. She reclined in the bride-chamber. She ate of the banquet for which she had hungered. . . . She found what she had sought.[50]

Those who are gnostics follow her path. But non-gnostic Christians "do not seek":

> . . . these—the ones who are ignorant—do not seek after God. . . . they do not inquire about God . . . the senseless man hears the call, but he is ignorant of the place to which he has been called. And he did not ask, during the preaching, "Where is the temple into which I should go and worship?"[51]

Those who merely believe the preaching they hear, without asking questions, and who accept the worship set before them, not only remain ignorant themselves, but "if they find someone else who asks about his salvation,"[52] they act immediately to censor and silence him.

Second, these "enemies" assert that they themselves are the soul's "shepherd":

> . . . They did not realize that she has an invisible, spiritual body; they think "We are her shepherd, who feeds her." But they did not realize that she knows another way which is hidden from them. This her true shepherd taught her in *gnosis*.[53]

Using the common term for bishop (*poimen*, "shepherd"), the author refers, apparently, to members of the clergy: they did not know that the gnostic Christian had direct access to Christ himself, the soul's true shepherd, and did not need their guidance. Nor did these would-be shepherds realize that the true church was not the visible one (the community over which they preside), but that "she has an invisible, spiritual body"[54]—that is, she included only those who were spiritual. Only Christ, and they themselves, knew who they were. Furthermore, these "outsiders" indulged themselves in drinking wine, in sexual activity, and they worked at ordinary business, like pagans. To justify their conduct, they oppressed and slandered those who had attained *gnosis*, and who practiced total renunciation. The gnostic declares:

> . . . we take no interest in them when they [malign] us. And we ignore them when they curse us. When they cast shame in our face, we look at them, and do not speak. For they work at their business, but we go around in hunger and thirst . . .[55]

These "enemies," I submit, were following the kind of advice that orthodox leaders like Irenaeus, Tertullian, and Hippolytus prescribed for dealing with heretics. In the first place, they refused to question the rule of faith and common doctrine. Tertullian warns that "the heretics and the philosophers" both ask the same questions, and urges believers to dismiss them all:

> Away with all attempts to produce a mixed Christianity of Stoic, Platonic, or dialectic composition! We want no curious disputation after possessing Christ Jesus, no inquiring after enjoying the gospel! With our faith, we desire no further belief.[56]

He complains that heretics welcome anyone to join with them, "for they do not care how differently they treat topics," so long as they meet together to approach "the city of the one sole truth."[57] Yet their metaphor indicates that the gnostics were neither relativists nor skeptics. Like the orthodox, they sought the "one sole truth." But gnostics tended to regard all doctrines, speculations, and myths—their own as well as others'—only as approaches to truth. The orthodox, by contrast, were coming to identify their own doctrine as itself the truth—the sole legitimate form of Christian faith. Tertullian admits that the heretics claimed to follow Jesus' counsel ("Seek, and you shall find; knock, and it shall be opened to you").[58] But this means, he says, that Christ taught "one definite thing"—what the rule of faith contains. Once having found and believed this, the Christian has nothing further to seek:

> Away with the person who is seeking where he never finds; for he seeks where nothing can be found. Away with him who is always knocking; because it will never be opened to him, for he knocks where there is no one to open. Away with the one who is always asking, because he will never be heard, for he asks of one who does not hear.[59]

Irenaeus agrees: "According to this course of procedure, one would be always inquiring, but never finding, because he has rejected the very method of discovery."[60] The only safe and accurate course, he says, is to accept in faith what the church teaches, recognizing the limits of human understanding.

As we have seen, these "enemies" of the gnostics followed the church fathers' advice in asserting the claims of the clergy over gnostic Christians. Also, they treated "unrepentant" gnostics as outsiders to Christian faith; and finally, they affirmed the value of ordinary employment and family life over the demands of radical asceticism.

While catholic Christians and radical gnostics took opposite stands, each claiming to represent the church, and each denouncing the others as heretics, the Valentinians took a mediating position. Resisting the orthodox attempt to label them as outsiders, they identified themselves as fully members of the church. But the Valentinians engaged in vehement debate among themselves over the opposite question—the status of *catholic* Christians. So serious was their disagreement over this question that the crisis finally split the followers of Valentinus into two different factions.

Were catholic Christians included in the church, the "body of Christ"? The Eastern branch of Valentinians said *no*. They maintained that Christ's body, the church, was "purely spiritual," consisting only of those who were spiritual, who had received *gnosis*. Theodotus, the great teacher of the Eastern school, defined the church as "the chosen race,"[61] those "chosen before the foundation of the world."[62] Their salvation was certain, predestined—and exclusive. Like Tertullian in his later years, Theodotus taught that only those who received direct spiritual inspiration belonged to the "spiritual church."[63]

But Ptolemy and Heracleon, the leading teachers of the Western school of Valentinians, disagreed. Against Theodotus, they claimed that "Christ's body," the church, consisted of two distinct elements, one spiritual, the other unspiritual. This meant, they explained, that *both* gnostic and non-gnostic Christians stood within the same church. Citing Jesus' saying that "many are called, but few are chosen," they explained that Christians who lacked *gnosis*—by far the majority—were the many who were called. They themselves, as gnostic Christians, belonged to the few who were chosen. Heracleon taught that God had given them spiritual understanding for the sake of the rest—so that they would be able to teach "the many" and bring them to *gnosis*.[64]

The gnostic teacher Ptolemy agreed: Christ combined

within the church both spiritual and unspiritual Christians so that eventually all may become spiritual.[65] Meanwhile, both belonged to one church; both were baptized; both shared in the celebration of the mass; both made the same confession. What differentiated them was the level of their understanding. Uninitiated Christians mistakenly worshiped the creator, as if he were God; they believed in Christ as the one who would save them from sin, and who they believed had risen bodily from the dead: they accepted him by faith, but without understanding the mystery of his nature—or their own. But those who had gone on to receive *gnosis* had come to recognize Christ as the one sent from the Father of Truth, whose coming revealed to them that their own nature was identical with his—and with God's.

To illustrate their relationship, Heracleon offers a symbolic interpretation of the church as a temple: those who were ordinary Christians, not yet gnostics, worshiped like the Levites, in the temple courtyard, shut out from the mystery. Only those who had *gnosis* might enter within the "holy of holies," which signified the place "where those who are spiritual worship God." Yet one temple—the church—embraced both places of worship.[66]

The Valentinian author of the *Interpretation of the Knowledge* agrees with this view. He explains that although Jesus came into the world and died for the sake of the "church of mortals,"[67] now this church, the "place of faith," was split and divided into factions.[68] Some members had received spiritual gifts—power to heal, prophecy, above all, *gnosis*; others had not.

This gnostic teacher expresses concern that this situation often caused hostility and misunderstanding. Those who were spiritually advanced tended to withdraw from those they considered "ignorant" Christians, and hesitated to share their insights with them. Those who lacked spiritual inspiration envied those who spoke out in public at the worship service and who spoke in prophecy, taught, and healed others.[69]

The author addresses the whole community as he attempts to reconcile both gnostic and non-gnostic Christians with one another. Drawing upon a traditional metaphor, he reminds them that all believers are members of the church, the "body of Christ." First he recalls Paul's words:

> For just as the body is one and has many members, and all the members of the body, though many, are one body, so it is with Christ. . . . The eye cannot say to the hand, "I have no need of you," nor again the head to the feet, "I have no need of you."[70]

Then he goes on to preach to those who feel inferior, lacking spiritual powers, who are not yet gnostic initiates:

> . . . Do not accuse your Head [Christ] because it has not made you as an eye, but a finger; and do not be jealous of what has been made an eye or a hand or a foot, but be thankful that you are not outside the body.[71]

To those who are spiritual, who have *gnosis*, and who have received "gifts," he says:

> . . . Does someone have a prophetic gift? Share it without hesitation. Do not approach your brother with jealousy . . . How do you know [that someone] is ignorant? . . . [You] are ignorant when you [hate them] and are jealous of them.[72]

Like Paul, he urges all members to love one another, to work and suffer together, mature and immature Christians alike, gnostics and ordinary believers, and so "to share in the (true) harmony."[73] According to the Western school of Valentinian gnostics, then, "the church" included the community of catholic Christians, but was not limited to it. Most Christians, they claimed, did not even perceive the most important element of the church, the spiritual element, which consisted of all who had *gnosis*.

From the bishop's viewpoint, of course, the gnostic position was outrageous. These heretics challenged his right to define what he considered to be his own church; they had the audacity to debate whether or not catholic Christians participated; and they claimed that their own group formed the essential nucleus, the "spiritual church." Rejecting such religious elitism, orthodox leaders attempted instead to construct a *universal* church. Desiring to open that church to everyone, they welcomed members from every social class, every racial or cultural origin, whether educated or illiterate—everyone, that is, who would submit to their system of organization. The bishops drew the line against those who challenged any of the three elements of this system: doctrine, ritual, and clerical hierarchy—and the gnostics challenged them all. Only by suppressing gnosticism did orthodox leaders establish that system of organization which united all believers into a single institutional structure. They allowed no other distinction between first- and second-class members than that between the clergy and the laity, nor did they tolerate any who claimed exemption from doctrinal conformity, from ritual participation, and from obedience to the discipline that priests and bishops administered. Gnostic churches, which rejected that system for more subjective forms of religious affiliation, survived, as churches, for only a few hundred years.

CHAPTER VI

Gnosis: Self=Knowledge as Knowledge of God

> ... Thomas said to him, "Lord, we do not know where you are going; how can we know the way?" Jesus said to him, "I am the way, the truth, and the life; no one comes to the Father, but by me."[1]

THE GOSPEL OF JOHN, which contains this saying, is a remarkable book that many gnostic Christians claimed for themselves and used as a primary source for gnostic teaching.[2] Yet the emerging church, despite some orthodox opposition, included John within the New Testament. What makes John acceptably "orthodox"? Why did the church accept John while rejecting such writings as the *Gospel of Thomas* or the *Dialogue of the Savior*? In considering this question, remember that anyone who drives through the United States is likely to see billboards proclaiming this saying from John— billboards signed by any of the local churches. Their purpose is clear: by indicating that one finds God only through Jesus, the saying, in its contemporary context, implies that one finds Jesus only through the church. Similarly, in the first centuries of this era, Christians concerned to strengthen the institutional church could find support in John.

Gnostic sources offer a different religious perspective. According to the *Dialogue of the Savior*, for example, when the disciples asked Jesus the same question ("What is the place to which we shall go?") he answered, "the place which you can reach, stand there!"[3] The *Gospel of Thomas* relates that when the disciples asked Jesus where they should go, he said only, "There is light within a man of light, and it lights up the whole world. If he does not shine, he is darkness."[4] Far from legitimizing any institution, both sayings direct one instead to oneself—to one's inner capacity to find one's own direction, to the "light within."

The contrast sketched above is, of course, somewhat simplistic. Followers of Valentinus themselves demonstrated—convincingly—that many sayings and stories in John could lend themselves to such interpretation. But Christians like Irenaeus apparently decided that, on balance, the gospel of John (especially, perhaps, when placed in sequence after Matthew, Mark, and Luke) could serve the needs of the emerging institution.

As the church organized politically, it could sustain within itself many contradictory ideas and practices as long as the disputed elements supported its basic institutional structure. In the third and fourth centuries, for example, hundreds of catholic Christians adopted ascetic forms of self-discipline, seeking religious insight through solitude, visions, and ecstatic experience. (The terms "monk" and "monastic" come from the Greek word *monachos*, meaning "solitary," or "single one," which the *Gospel of Thomas* frequently uses to describe the gnostic.) Rather than exclude the monastic movement, the church moved, in the fourth century, to bring the monks into line with episcopal authority. The scholar Frederik Wisse has suggested that the monks who lived at the monastery of St. Pachomius, within sight of the cliff where the texts were found, may have included the Nag Hammadi texts within their devotional library.[5] But in 367, when Athanasius, the powerful Archbishop of Alexandria, sent an order to purge all "apocryphal books" with "heretical" tendencies, one (or several) of the monks may have hidden the precious manuscripts in the jar and buried it on the cliff of the Jabal al-Ṭārif, where Muḥammad 'Alī found it 1,600 years later.

Furthermore, as the church, disparate as it was internally, increasingly became a political unity between 150 and 400, its leaders tended to treat their opponents—an even more diverse range of groups—as if they, too, constituted an *opposite* political unity. When Irenaeus denounced the heretics as "gnostics,"[6] he referred less to any specific doctrinal agreement among them (indeed, he often castigated them for the variety of their beliefs) than to the fact that they all resisted accepting the authority of the clergy, the creed, and the New Testament canon.

What—if anything—did the various groups that Irenaeus called "gnostic" have in common? Or, to put the question another way, what do the diverse texts discovered at Nag Hammadi have in common? No simple answer could cover all the different groups that the orthodox attack, or all the different texts in the Nag Hammadi collection. But I suggest that the trouble with gnosticism, from the orthodox viewpoint, was not only that gnostics often disagreed with the majority on such specific issues as those we have explored so far—the organization of authority, the participation of women, martyrdom: the orthodox recognized that those they called "gnostics" shared a fundamental religious perspective that remained antithetical to the claims of the institutional church.

For orthodox Christians insisted that humanity needs a way beyond its own power—a divinely given way—to approach God. And this, they declared, the catholic church offered to those who would be lost without it: "Outside the church there is no salvation." Their conviction was based on the premise that God created humanity. As Irenaeus says, "In this respect God differs from humanity; God makes, but humanity is made."[7] One is the originating agent, the other the passive recipient; one is "truly perfect in all things,"[8] omnipotent, infinite, the other an imperfect and finite creature. The philosopher Justin Martyr says that when he recognized the great difference between the human mind and God, he abandoned Plato and became a

Christian philosopher. He relates that before his conversion an old man challenged his basic assumption, asking, "What affinity, then, is there between us and God? Is the soul also divine and immortal, and a part of that very regal mind?" Speaking as a disciple of Plato, Justin answered without hesitation, "Certainly."⁹ But when the old man's further questions led him to doubt that certainty, he says he realized that the human mind could not find God within itself and needed instead to be enlightened by divine revelation—by means of the Scriptures and the faith proclaimed in the church.

But some gnostic Christians went so far as to claim that humanity created God—and so, from its own inner potential, discovered for itself the revelation of truth. This conviction may underlie the ironic comment in the *Gospel of Philip*:

> . . . God created humanity; [but now human beings] create God. That is the way it is in the world—human beings make gods, and worship their creation. It would be appropriate for the gods to worship human beings!¹⁰

The gnostic Valentinus taught that humanity itself manifests the divine life and divine revelation. The church, he says, consists of that portion of humanity that recognizes and celebrates its divine origin.¹¹ But Valentinus did not use the term in its contemporary sense, to refer to the human race taken collectively. Instead, he and his followers thought of *Anthropos* (here translated "humanity") as the underlying nature of that collective entity, the archetype, or spiritual essence, of human being. In this sense, some of Valentinus' followers, "those . . . considered more skillful"¹² than the rest, agreed with the teacher Colorbasus, who said that when God revealed himself, He revealed himself in the form of *Anthropos*. Still others, Irenaeus reports, maintained that

> the primal father of the whole, the primal beginning, and the primal incomprehensible, is called *Anthropos* . . . and that this is the great and abstruse mystery, namely, that the

power which is above all others, and contains all others in its embrace, is called *Anthropos*.[13]

For this reason, these gnostics explained, the Savior called himself "Son of Man" (that is, Son of *Anthropos*).[14] The Sethian gnostics, who called the creator Ialdabaoth (a name apparently derived from mystical Judaism but which here indicates his inferior status), said that for this reason, when the creator,

> Ialdabaoth, becoming arrogant in spirit, boasted himself over all those who were below him, and explained, "I am father, and God, and above me there is no one," his mother, hearing him speak thus, cried out against him: "Do not lie, Ialdabaoth; for the father of all, the primal *Anthropos*, is above you; and so is *Anthropos*, the son of *Anthropos*.[15]

In the words of another Valentinian, since human beings created the whole language of religious expression, so, in effect, humanity created the divine world: ". . . and this [*Anthropos*] is really he who is God over all."

Many gnostics, then, would have agreed in principle with Ludwig Feuerbach, the nineteenth-century psychologist, that "theology is really anthropology" (the term derives, of course, from *anthropos*, and means "study of humanity"). For gnostics, exploring the *psyche* became explicitly what it is for many people today implicitly—a religious quest. Some who seek their own interior direction, like the radical gnostics, reject religious institutions as a hindrance to their progress. Others, like the Valentinians, willingly participate in them, although they regard the church more as an instrument of their own self-discovery than as the necessary "ark of salvation."

Besides defining God in opposite ways, gnostic and orthodox Christians diagnosed the human condition very differently. The orthodox followed traditional Jewish teaching that what separates humanity from God, besides the essential dissimilarity, is human sin. The New Testament term for sin, *hamartia*, comes from the sport of archery; literally, it means "missing the mark."

New Testament sources teach that we suffer distress, mental and physical, because we fail to achieve the moral goal toward which we aim: "all have sinned, and fall short of the glory of God."[16] So, according to the gospel of Mark, when Jesus came to reconcile God and humanity, he announced: "The time is fulfilled, and the kingdom of God is at hand; repent, and believe in the gospel."[17] Mark announces that Jesus alone could offer healing and forgiveness of sins; only those who receive his message in faith experience deliverance. The gospel of John expresses the desperate situation of humanity apart from the Savior:

> For God sent the Son into the world . . . that the world might be saved through him. He who believes in him is not condemned; he who does not believe is condemned already, because he has not believed in the name of the only Son of God.[18]

Many gnostics, on the contrary, insisted that ignorance, not sin, is what involves a person in suffering. The gnostic movement shared certain affinities with contemporary methods of exploring the self through psychotherapeutic techniques. Both gnosticism and psychotherapy value, above all, knowledge—the self-knowledge which is insight. They agree that, lacking this, a person experiences the sense of being driven by impulses he does not understand. Valentinus expressed this in a myth. He tells how the world originated when Wisdom, the Mother of all beings, brought it forth out of her own suffering. The four elements that Greek philosophers said constituted the world—earth, air, fire, and water—are concrete forms of her experiences:

> Thus the earth arose from her confusion, water from her terror; air from the consolidation of her grief; while fire . . . was inherent in all these elements . . . as ignorance lay concealed in these three sufferings.[19]

Thus the world was born out of suffering. (The Greek word *pathos*, here translated "suffering," also connotes being the passive recipient, not the initiator, of one's experience.) Valentinus or one of his followers tells a different version of the myth in the *Gospel of Truth*:

> . . . Ignorance . . . brought about anguish and terror. And the anguish grew solid like a fog, so that no one was able to see. For this reason error is powerful . . .[20]

Most people live, then, in oblivion—or, in contemporary terms, in unconsciousness. Remaining unaware of their own selves, they have "no root."[21] The *Gospel of Truth* describes such existence as a nightmare. Those who live in it experience "terror and confusion and instability and doubt and division," being caught in "many illusions."[22] So, according to the passage scholars call the "nightmare parable," they lived

> as if they were sunk in sleep and found themselves in disturbing dreams. Either (there is) a place to which they are fleeing, or, without strength, they come (from) having chased after others, or they are involved in striking blows, or they are receiving blows themselves, or they have fallen from high places, or they take off into the air though they do not even have wings. Again, sometimes (it is as) if people were murdering them, though there is no one even pursuing them, or they themselves are killing their neighbors, for they have been stained with their blood. When those who are going through all these things wake up, they see nothing, they who were in the midst of these disturbances, for they are nothing. Such is the way of those who have cast ignorance aside as sleep, leaving [its works] behind like a dream in the night. . . . This is the way everyone has acted, as though asleep at the time when he was ignorant. And this is the way he has come to knowledge, as if he had awakened.[23]

Whoever remains ignorant, a "creature of oblivion,"[24] cannot experience fulfillment. Gnostics said that such a person "dwells in deficiency" (the opposite of fulfillment). For deficiency consists of ignorance:

> . . . As with someone's ignorance, when he comes to have knowledge, his ignorance vanishes by itself; as the

darkness vanishes when light appears, so also the deficiency vanishes in the fulfillment.[25]

Self-ignorance is also a form of self-destruction. According to the *Dialogue of the Savior*, whoever does not understand the elements of the universe, and of himself, is bound for annihilation:

> . . . If one does not [understand] how the fire came to be, he will burn in it, because he does not know his root. If one does not first understand the water, he does not know anything. . . . If one does not understand how the wind that blows came to be, he will run with it. If one does not understand how the body that he wears came to be, he will perish with it. . . . Whoever does not understand how he came will not understand how he will go . . .[26]

How—or where—is one to seek self-knowledge? Many gnostics share with psychotherapy a second major premise: both agree—against orthodox Christianity—that the psyche bears *within itself* the potential for liberation or destruction. Few psychiatrists would disagree with the saying attributed to Jesus in the *Gospel of Thomas*:

> "If you bring forth what is within you, what you bring forth will save you. If you do not bring forth what is within you, what you do not bring forth will destroy you."[27]

Such insight comes gradually, through effort: "Recognize what is before your eyes, and what is hidden will be revealed to you."[28] Such gnostics acknowledged that pursuing *gnosis* engages each person in a solitary, difficult process, as one struggles against internal resistance. They characterized this resistance to *gnosis* as the desire to sleep or to be drunk—that is, to remain unconscious. So Jesus (who elsewhere says "I am the knowledge of the truth")[29] declares that when he came into the world

> I found them all drunk; I found none of them thirsty. And my soul became afflicted for the sons of men, because they are blind in their hearts and do not have sight; for empty they came into this world, and empty they seek to leave this world. But for the moment they are drunk.[30]

Gnosis: Self-Knowledge as Knowledge of God

The teacher Silvanus, whose *Teachings*[31] were discovered at Nag Hammadi, encourages his followers to resist unconsciousness:

> ... end the sleep which weighs heavy upon you. Depart from the oblivion which fills you with darkness ... Why do you pursue the darkness, though the light is available for you? ... Wisdom calls you, yet you desire foolishness. ... a foolish man ... goes the ways of the desire of every passion. He swims in the desires of life and has foundered. ... he is like a ship which the wind tosses to and fro, and like a loose horse which has no rider. For this (one) needed the rider, which is reason. ... before everything else ... know yourself ...[32]

The *Gospel of Thomas* also warns that self-discovery involves inner turmoil:

> Jesus said, "Let him who seeks continue seeking until he finds. When he finds, he will become troubled. When he becomes troubled, he will be astonished, and he will rule over all things."[33]

What is the source of the "light" discovered within? Like Freud, who professed to follow the "light of reason," most gnostic sources agreed that "the lamp of the body is the mind"[34] (a saying which the *Dialogue of the Savior* attributes to Jesus). Silvanus, the teacher, says:

> ... Bring in your guide and your teacher. The mind is the guide, but reason is the teacher. ... Live according to your mind ... Acquire strength, for the mind is strong ... Enlighten your mind ... Light the lamp within you.[35]

To do this, Silvanus continues,

> Knock on yourself as upon a door and walk upon yourself as on a straight road. For if you walk on the road, it is impossible for you to go astray. ... Open the door for yourself that you may know what is ... Whatever you will open for yourself, you will open.[36]

The *Gospel of Truth* expresses the same thought:

> . . . If one has knowledge, he receives what is his own, and draws it to himself . . . Whoever is to have knowledge in this way knows where he comes from, and where he is going.[37]

The *Gospel of Truth* also expresses this in metaphor: each person must receive "his own name"—not, of course, one's ordinary name, but one's true identity. Those who are "the sons of interior knowledge"[38] gain the power to speak their own names. The gnostic teacher addresses them:

> . . . Say, then, from the heart that you are the perfect day, and in you dwells the light that does not fail. . . . For you are the understanding that is drawn forth. . . . Be concerned with yourselves; do not be concerned with other things which you have rejected from yourselves.[39]

So, according to the *Gospel of Thomas*, Jesus ridiculed those who thought of the "Kingdom of God" in literal terms, as if it were a specific place: "If those who lead you say to you, 'Look, the Kingdom is in the sky,' then the birds will arrive there before you. If they say to you, 'It is in the sea,' " then, he says, the fish will arrive before you. Instead, it is a state of self-discovery:

> ". . . Rather, the Kingdom is inside of you, and it is outside of you. When you come to know yourselves, then you will be known, and you will realize that you are the sons of the living Father. But if you will not know yourselves, then you dwell in poverty, and it is you who *are* that poverty."[40]

But the disciples, mistaking that "Kingdom" for a future event, persisted in their questioning:

> His disciples said to him, "When will . . . the new world come?" He said to them, "What you look forward to has already come, but you do not recognize it." . . . His disciples said to him, "When will the Kingdom come?"

⟨Jesus said,⟩ "It will not come by waiting for it. It will not be a matter of saying 'Here it is' or 'There it is.' Rather, the Kingdom of the Father is spread out upon the earth, and men do not see it."[41]

That "Kingdom," then, symbolizes a state of transformed consciousness:

Jesus saw infants being suckled. He said to his disciples, "These infants being suckled are like those who enter the Kingdom." They said to him, "Shall we, then, as children, enter the Kingdom?" Jesus said to them, "When you make the two one, and when you make the inside like the outside and the outside like the inside, and the above like the below, and when you make the male and the female one and the same . . . then you will enter [the Kingdom]."[42]

Yet what the "living Jesus" of Thomas rejects as naïve—the idea that the Kingdom of God is an actual event expected in history—is the notion of the Kingdom that the synoptic gospels of the New Testament most often attribute to Jesus as his teaching. According to Matthew, Luke, and Mark, Jesus proclaimed the coming Kingdom of God, when captives shall gain their freedom, when the diseased shall recover, the oppressed shall be released, and harmony shall prevail over the whole world. Mark says that the disciples expected the Kingdom to come as a cataclysmic event in their own lifetime, since Jesus had said that some of them would live to see "the kingdom of God come with power."[43] Before his arrest, Mark says, Jesus warned that although "the end is not yet,"[44] they must expect it at any time. All three gospels insist that the Kingdom will come in the near future (though they also contain many passages indicating that it is here already). Luke makes Jesus say explicitly "the kingdom of God is within you."[45] Some gnostic Christians, extending that type of interpretation, expected human liberation to occur not through actual events in history, but through internal transformation.

For similar reasons, gnostic Christians criticized orthodox

views of Jesus that identified him as one external to the disciples, and superior to them. For, according to Mark, when the disciples came to recognize who Jesus was, they thought of him as their appointed King:

> And Jesus went on with his disciples to the villages of Caesarea Philippi; and on the way he asked his disciples, "Who do men say that I am?" And they told him, "John the Baptist; and others say, Elijah; and others one of the prophets." And he asked them, "But who do you say that I am?" Peter answered him, "You are the Christ."[46]

Matthew adds to this that Jesus blessed Peter for the accuracy of his recognition, and declared immediately that the church shall be founded upon Peter, and upon his recognition of Jesus as the Messiah. One of the earliest of all Christian confessions states simply, "Jesus is Lord!" But *Thomas* tells the story differently:

> Jesus said to his disciples, "Compare me to someone and tell me whom I am like." Simon Peter said to him, "You are like a righteous angel." Matthew said to him, "You are like a wise philosopher." Thomas said to him, "Master, my mouth is wholly incapable of saying whom you are like." Jesus said, "I am not your master. Because you have drunk, you have become drunk from the bubbling stream which I have measured out."[48]

Here Jesus does not deny his role as Messiah or as teacher, at least in relation to Peter and Matthew. But here they—and their answers—represent an inferior level of understanding. Thomas, who recognizes that he cannot assign any specific role to Jesus, transcends, at this moment of recognition, the relation of student to master. He becomes himself like the "living Jesus," who declares, "Whoever will drink from my mouth will become as I am, and I myself will become that person, and the things that are hidden will be revealed to him."[49]

Gnostic sources often do depict Jesus answering questions, taking the role of teacher, revealer, and spiritual master. But here, too, the gnostic model stands close to the psychotherapeutic one. Both acknowledge the need for guidance, but only as a provisional measure. The purpose of accepting authority is to learn to outgrow it. When one becomes mature, one no longer needs any external authority. The one who formerly took the place of a disciple comes to recognize himself as Jesus' "twin brother." Who, then, is Jesus the teacher? *Thomas the Contender* identifies him simply as "the knowledge of the truth."[50] According to the *Gospel of Thomas*, Jesus refused to validate the experience that the disciples must discover for themselves:

> They said to him, "Tell us who you are so that we may believe in you." He said to them, "You read the face of the sky and of the earth, but you have not recognized the one who is before you, and you do not know how to read this moment."[51]

And when, in frustration, they asked him, "Who are you, that you should say these things to us?" Jesus, instead of answering, criticized their question: "You do not realize who I am from what I say to you."[52] We noted already that, according to *Thomas*, when the disciples asked Jesus to show them where he was so that they might reach that place as well, he refused, directing them instead to themselves, to discover the resources hidden within. The same theme occurs in the *Dialogue of the Savior*. As Jesus talks with his three chosen disciples, Matthew asks him to show him the "place of life," which is, he says, the "pure light." Jesus answers, "Every one [of you] who has known himself has seen it."[53] Here again, he deflects the question, pointing the disciple instead toward his own self-discovery. When the disciples, expecting him to reveal secrets to them, ask Jesus, "Who is the one who seeks, [and who is the one who] reveals?"[54] he answers that the one who seeks the truth—the disciple—is also the one who reveals it. Since Matthew persists in asking him questions, Jesus says that he does not know the answer himself, "nor have I heard about it, except from you."[55]

The disciple who comes to know himself can discover, then, what even Jesus cannot teach. The *Testimony of Truth* says that the gnostic becomes a "disciple of his [own] mind,"[56] discovering that his own mind "is the father of the truth."[57] He learns what he needs to know by himself in meditative silence. Consequently, he considers himself equal to everyone, maintaining his own independence of anyone else's authority: "And he is patient with everyone; he makes himself equal to everyone, and he also separates himself from them."[58] Silvanus, too, regards "your mind" as "a guiding principle." Whoever follows the direction of his own mind need not accept anyone else's advice:

> Have a great number of friends, but not counselors.
> . . . But if you do acquire [a friend], do not entrust yourself
> to him. Entrust yourself to God alone as father and as
> friend.[59]

Finally, those gnostics who conceived of *gnosis* as a subjective, immediate experience, concerned themselves above all with the internal significance of events. Here again they diverged from orthodox tradition, which maintained that human destiny depends upon the events of "salvation history"—the history of Israel, especially the prophets' predictions of Christ and then his actual coming, his life, and his death and resurrection. All of the New Testament gospels, whatever their differences, concern themselves with Jesus as a historical person. And all of them rely on the prophets' predictions to prove the validity of the Christian message. Matthew, for example, continually repeats the refrain, "This was done to fulfill what was spoken by the prophets."[60] Justin, too, attempting to persuade the emperor of the truth of Christianity, points as proof toward the fulfillment of prophecy: "And this indeed you can see for yourselves, and be convinced of by fact."[61] But according to the *Gospel of Thomas*, Jesus dismisses as irrelevant the prophets' predictions:

> His disciples said to him, "Twenty-four prophets spoke
> in Israel, and all of them spoke in you." He said to them,
> "You have ignored the one living in your presence, and
> have spoken (only) of the dead."[62]

Such gnostic Christians saw actual events as secondary to their perceived meaning.

For this reason, this type of gnosticism shares with psychotherapy a fascination with the nonliteral significance of language, as both attempt to understand the internal quality of experience. The psychoanalyst C. C. Jung has interpreted Valentinus' creation myth as a description of the psychological processes. Valentinus tells how all things originate from "the depth," the "abyss"[63]—in psychoanalytic terms, from the unconscious. From that "depth" emerge Mind and Truth, and from them, in turn, the Word (Logos) and Life. And it was the word that brought humanity into being. Jung read this as a mythical account of the origin of human consciousness.

A psychoanalyst might find significance as well in the continuation of this myth, as Valentinus tells how Wisdom, youngest daughter of the primal Couple, was seized by a passion to know the Father which she interpreted as love. Her attempts to know him would have led her to self-destruction had she not encountered a power called The Limit, "a power which supports all things and preserves them,"[64] which freed her of emotional turmoil and restored her to her original place.

A follower of Valentinus, the author of the *Gospel of Philip*, explores the relationship of experiential truth to verbal description. He says that "truth brought names into existence in the world because it is not possible to teach it without names."[65] But truth must be clothed in symbols: "Truth did not come into the world naked, but it came in types and images. One will not receive truth in any other way."[66] This gnostic teacher criticizes those who mistake religious language for a literal language, professing faith in God, in Christ, in the resurrection or the church, as if these were all "things" external to themselves. For, he explains, in ordinary speech, each word refers to a specific, external phenomenon; a person "sees the sun without being a sun, and he sees the sky and the earth and everything else, but he is not these things."[67] Religious language, on the other hand, is a language of internal transformation; whoever perceives divine reality "becomes what he sees":

> . . . You saw the spirit, you became spirit. You saw Christ, you became Christ. You saw [the Father, you] shall become Father. . . . you see yourself, and what you see you shall [become].[68]

Whoever achieves *gnosis* becomes "no longer a Christian, but a Christ."[69]

We can see, then, that such gnosticism was more than a protest movement against orthodox Christianity. Gnosticism also included a religious perspective that implicitly opposed the development of the kind of institution that became the early catholic church. Those who expected to "become Christ" themselves were not likely to recognize the institutional structures of the church—its bishop, priest, creed, canon, or ritual—as bearing ultimate authority.

This religious perspective differentiates gnosticism not only from orthodoxy, but also, for all the similarities, from psychotherapy, for most members of the psychotherapeutic profession follow Freud in refusing to attribute real existence to the figments of imagination. They do not regard their attempt to discover what is within the psyche as equivalent to discovering the secrets of the universe. But many gnostics, like many artists, search for interior self-knowledge as the key to understanding universal truths—"who we are, where we came from, where we go." According to the *Book of Thomas the Contender*, "whoever has not known himself has known nothing, but he who has known himself has at the same time already achieved knowledge about the depths of all things."[70]

This conviction—that whoever explores human experience simultaneously discovers divine reality—is one of the elements that marks gnosticism as a distinctly religious movement. Simon Magus, Hippolytus reports, claimed that each human being is a dwelling place, "and that in him dwells an infinite power . . . the root of the universe."[71] But since that infinite power exists in two modes, one actual, the other potential, so this infinite power "exists in a latent condition in everyone," but "potentially, not actually."[72]

How is one to realize that potential? Many of the gnostic sources cited so far contain only aphorisms directing the disciple to search for knowledge, but refraining from telling anyone how to search. Discovering that for oneself is, apparently, the first step toward self-knowledge. Thus, in the *Gospel of Thomas*, the disciples ask Jesus to tell them what to do:

> His disciples questioned him and said to him, "Do you want us to fast? How shall we pray? Shall we give alms? What diet shall we observe?" Jesus said, "Do not tell lies, and do not do what you hate . . ."[73]

His ironic answer turns them back to themselves: who but one-self can judge when one is lying or what one hates? Such cryptic answers earned sharp criticism from Plotinus, the neo-Platonic philosopher who attacked the gnostics when their teaching was attracting some of his own students away from philosophy. Plotinus complained that the gnostics had no program for teaching: "They say only, 'Look to God!,' but they do not tell anyone *where* or *how* to look."[74]

Yet several of the sources discovered at Nag Hammadi do describe techniques of spiritual discipline. *Zostrianos*, the longest text in the Nag Hammadi library, tells how one spiritual master attained enlightenment, implicitly setting out a program for others to follow. Zostrianos relates that, first, he had to remove from himself physical desires, probably by ascetic practices. Second, he had to reduce "chaos in mind,"[75] stilling his mind with meditation. Then, he says, "after I set myself straight, I saw the perfect child"[76]—a vision of the divine presence. Later, he says, "I was pondering these matters in order to understand them. . . . I did not cease seeking a place of rest worthy of my spirit . . ."[77] But then, becoming "deeply troubled," discouraged with his progress, he went out into the desert, half anticipating being killed by wild animals. There, Zostrianos relates, he first

[135]

received a vision of "the messenger of the knowledge of the eternal Light,"[78] and went on to experience many other visions, which he relates in order to encourage others: "Why are you hesitating? Seek when you are sought; when you are invited, listen. . . . Look at the Light. Flee the darkness. Do not be led astray to your destruction."[79]

Other gnostic sources offer more specific directions. The *Discourse on the Eighth and the Ninth* discloses an "order of tradition" that guides the ascent to higher knowledge. Written in dialogue form, the *Discourse* opens as the student reminds his spiritual master of a promise:

> "[O my father], yesterday you promised me [that you would bring] my mind into [the] eighth and afterwards you would bring me into the ninth. You said that this is the order of the tradition."[80]

His teacher assents: "O my son, indeed this is the order. But the promise was according to human nature."[81] He explains that the disciple himself must bring forth the understanding he seeks: "I set forth the action for you. But the understanding dwells in you. In me, (it is) as if the power were pregnant."[82] The disciple is astonished; is the power, then, actually within him? The master suggests that they both must pray that the disciple may come to the higher levels, the "eighth and the ninth." Already he has progressed through the first seven levels of understanding, impelled by moral effort and dedication. But the disciple admits that, so far, he has no firsthand experience of divine knowledge: "O my father, I understand nothing but the beauty which came to me in books."[83]

Now that he is ready to go beyond vicarious knowledge, the two join in prayer "to the perfect, invisible God to whom one speaks in silence."[84] The prayer moves into a chant of sacred words and vowels: "Zoxathazo a ōō ēē ōōō ēēē ōōōō ēē ōōōōōōōōōōō ōōōōō uuuuuu ōōōōōōōōōōōō ōōō Zozazoth."[85] After intoning the chant, the teacher prays, "Lord . . . acknowledge the spirit that is in us."[86] Then he enters into an ecstatic state:

> ". . . I see! I see indescribable depths. How shall I tell you, O my son? . . . How [shall I describe] the universe? I [am mind and] I see another mind, the one that [moves] the soul! I see the one that moves me from pure forgetfulness. You give me power! I see myself! I want to speak! Fear restrains me. I have found the beginning of the power that is above all powers, the one that has no beginning. . . . I have said, O my son, that I am Mind. I have seen! Language is not able to reveal this. For the entire eighth, O my son, and the souls that are in it, and the angels, sing a hymn in silence. And I, Mind, understand."[87]

Watching, the disciple himself is filled with ecstasy: "I rejoice, O my father, because I see you smiling. And the universe rejoices." Seeing his teacher as himself embodying the divine, the disciple pleads with him, "Let not my soul be deprived of the great divine vision. For everything is possible for you as master of the universe." The master tells him to sing in silence, and to "ask what you want in silence":

> When he had finished praising he shouted, "Father Trismegistus! What shall I say? We have received this light. And I myself see the same vision in you. I see the eighth and the souls that are in it and the angels singing a hymn to the ninth and its powers. . . . I pray to the end of the universe and the beginning of the beginning, to the object of man's quest, the immortal discovery . . . I am the instrument of thy spirit. Mind is thy plectrum. And thy counsel plucks me. I see myself! I have received power from thee. For thy love has reached us."[88]

The *Discourse* closes as the master instructs the student to write his experiences in a book (presumably the *Discourse* itself) to guide others who will "advance by stages, and enter into the way of immortality. . . . into the understanding of the eighth that reveals the ninth."[89]

. . .

Another extraordinary text, called *Allogenes*, which means "the stranger" (literally, "one from another race"), referring to the spiritually mature person who becomes a "stranger" to the world, also describes the stages of attaining *gnosis*. Here Messos, the initiate, at the first stage, learns of "the power that is within you." Allogenes explains to him his own process of spiritual development:

> . . . [I was] very disturbed, and [I] turned to myself. . . . [Having] seen the light that [surrounded] me and the good that was within me, I became divine.[90]

Then, Allogenes continues, he received a vision of a feminine power, Youel, "she who belongs to all the glories,"[91] who told him:

> . . . "Since your instruction has become complete, and you have known the good that is within you, hear concerning the Triple Power those things that you will guard in great silence and great mystery . . ."[92]

That power, paradoxically, is silent, although it utters sound: zza zza zza.[93] This, like the chant in the *Discourse*, suggests a meditative technique that includes intoning sound.

Having first discovered "the good . . . within me," Allogenes advanced to the second stage—to know oneself.

> [And then I] prayed that [the revelation] might occur to me. . . . I did not despair . . . I prepared myself therein, and I took counsel with myself for a hundred years. And I rejoiced exceedingly, since I was in a great light and a blessed path . . .[94]

Following this, Allogenes says, he had an experience out of the body, and saw "holy powers" that offered him specific instruction:

> . . . "O Allo[g]enes, behold your blessedness . . . in silence, wherein you know yourself as you are, and, seeking yourself, ascend to the Vitality that you will see moving. And if it is impossible for you to stand, fear nothing; but

if you wish to stand, ascend to the Existence, and you will find it standing and stilling itself . . . And when you receive a revelation . . . and you become afraid in that place, withdraw back because of the energies. And when you have become perfect in that place, still yourself."[95]

Is this speech of the "holy powers" to be recited in some dramatic performance enacted by members of the gnostic sect for the initiate in the course of ritual instruction? The text does not say, although the candidate goes on to describe his response:

Now I was listening to these things as those present spoke them. There was a stillness of silence within me, and I heard the blessedness whereby I knew myself as ⟨I am⟩.[96]

Following the instruction, the initiate says he was filled with "revelation . . . I received power . . . I knew the One who exists in me, and the Triple Power, and the revelation of his uncontainableness."[97] Ecstatic with this discovery, Allogenes desires to go further: "I was seeking the ineffable and Unknown God."[98] But at this point the "powers" tell Allogenes to cease in his futile attempt.

Contrary to many other gnostic sources, *Allogenes* teaches that, first, one can come to know "the good that is within," and second, to know oneself and "the one who exists within," but one cannot attain knowledge of the Unknown God. Any attempt to do so, to grasp the incomprehensible, hinders "the effortlessness which is within you." Instead, the initiate must content himself to hear about God "in accordance with the capacity provided by a primary revelation."[99] One's own experience and knowledge, then, essential for spiritual development, provides the basis for receiving understanding about God in *negative* form. *Gnosis* involves recognizing, finally, the limits of human knowledge:

". . . (Whoever) sees (God) as he is in every respect, or would say that he is something like *gnosis*, has sinned against him . . . because he did not know God."[100]

The powers instructed him "not [to] seek anything more, but go . . . It is not fitting to spend more time seeking."[101] Allogenes says he wrote this down for "the sake of those who will be worthy."[102] The detailed exposition of the initiate's experience, including sections of prayers, chants, instruction, punctuated by his retreat into meditation, suggest that the text records actual techniques of initiation for attaining that self-knowledge which is knowledge of divine power within.

But much of gnostic teaching on spiritual discipline remained, on principle, unwritten. For anyone can read what is written down—even those who are not "mature." Gnostic teachers usually reserved their secret instruction, sharing it only verbally, to ensure each candidate's suitability to receive it. Such instruction required each teacher to take responsibility for highly select, individualized attention to each candidate. And it required the candidate, in turn, to devote energy and time—often years—to the process. Tertullian sarcastically compares Valentinian initiation to that of the Eleusinian mysteries, which

> first beset all access to their group with tormenting conditions; and they require a long initiation before they enroll their members, even instruction for five years for their adept students, so that they may educate their opinions by this suspension of full knowledge, and, apparently, raise the value of their mysteries in proportion to the longing for them which they have created. Then follows the duty of silence . . .[103]

Obviously, such a program of discipline, like the higher levels of Buddhist teaching, would appeal only to a few. Although major themes of gnostic teaching, such as the discovery of the divine within, appealed to so many that they constituted a major threat to catholic doctrine, the religious perspectives and methods of gnosticism did not lend themselves to mass religion. In this respect, it was no match for the highly effective system of organization of the catholic church, which expressed a unified religious perspective based on the New Testament canon, offered a creed requiring the initiate to confess only the simplest essentials of faith, and celebrated rituals as simple and profound as baptism and the eucharist. The same basic framework of doctrine, ritual, and organization sustains nearly all Christian churches today, whether Roman Catholic, Orthodox, or Protestant. Without these elements, one can scarcely imagine how the Christian faith could have survived and attracted so many millions of adherents all over the world, throughout twenty centuries. For ideas alone do not make a religion powerful, although it cannot succeed without them; equally important are social and political structures that identify and unite people into a common affiliation.

CONCLUSION

I T IS THE WINNERS who write history—their way. No wonder,
then, that the viewpoint of the successful majority has
dominated all traditional accounts of the origin of Christianity. Ecclesiastical Christians first defined the terms (naming
themselves "orthodox" and their opponents "heretics"); then
they proceeded to demonstrate—at least to their own satisfaction
—that their triumph was historically inevitable, or, in religious
terms, "guided by the Holy Spirit."

But the discoveries at Nag Hammadi reopen fundamental
questions. They suggest that Christianity might have developed
in very different directions—or that Christianity as we know
it might not have survived at all. Had Christianity remained
multiform, it might well have disappeared from history, along
with dozens of rival religious cults of antiquity. I believe that we
owe the survival of Christian tradition to the organizational and
theological structure that the emerging church developed. Anyone as powerfully attracted to Christianity as I am will regard
that as a major achievement. We need not be surprised, then,

that the religious ideas enshrined in the creed (from "I believe in one God," who is "Father Almighty," and Christ's incarnation, death, and bodily resurrection "on the third day," to faith in the "holy, catholic, and apostolic church") coincide with social and political issues in the formation of orthodox Christianity.

Furthermore, since historians themselves tend to be intellectuals, it is, again, no surprise that most have interpreted the controversy between orthodox and gnostic Christians in terms of the "history of ideas," as if ideas, themselves assumed to be the essential mainspring of human action, battled (presumably in some disembodied state) for supremacy. So Tertullian, himself a highly intelligent man, fond of abstract thought, complained that "heretics and philosophers" concerned themselves with the same questions. The "questions that make people heretics"[1] are, he says, the following: Where does humanity come from, and how? Where does evil come from, and why? Tertullian insists (at least before his own violent break with the church) that the catholic church prevailed because it offered "truer" answers to these questions.

Yet the majority of Christians, gnostic and orthodox, like religious people of every tradition, concerned themselves with ideas primarily as expressions or symbols of religious experience. Such experience remains the source and testing ground of all religious ideas (as, for example, a man and a woman are likely to experience differently the idea that God is masculine). Gnosticism and orthodoxy, then, articulated very different kinds of human experience; I suspect that they appealed to different types of persons.

For when gnostic Christians inquired about the origin of evil they did not interpret the term, as we do, primarily in terms of moral evil. The Greek term *kakía* (like the English term "ill-ness") originally meant "what is bad"—what one desires to avoid, such as physical pain, sickness, suffering, misfortune, every kind of harm. When followers of Valentinus asked about the source of *kakía*, they referred especially to emotional harm—

fear, confusion, grief. According to the *Gospel of Truth*, the process of self-discovery begins as a person experiences the "anguish and terror"[2] of the human condition, as if lost in a fog or haunted in sleep by terrifying nightmares. Valentinus' myth of humanity's origin, as we have seen, describes the anticipation of death and destruction as the experiential beginning of the gnostic's search. "They say that all materiality was formed from three experiences [or: sufferings]: terror, pain, and confusion [*aporia*; literally, "roadlessness," not knowing where to go]."[3]

Since such experiences, especially the fear of death and dissolution, are located, in the first place, in the body, the gnostic tended to mistrust the body, regarding it as the saboteur that inevitably engaged him in suffering. Nor did the gnostic trust the blind forces that prevail in the universe; after all, these are the forces that constitute the body. What can bring release? Gnostics came to the conviction that the only way out of suffering was to realize the truth about humanity's place and destiny in the universe. Convinced that the only answers were to be found within, the gnostic engaged on an intensely private interior journey.

Whoever comes to experience his own nature—human nature—as itself the "source of all things," the primary reality, will receive enlightenment. Realizing the essential Self, the divine within, the gnostic laughed in joy at being released from external constraints to celebrate his identification with the divine being:

> The gospel of truth is a joy for those who have received from the Father of truth the grace of knowing him . . . For he discovered them in himself, and they discovered him in themselves, the incomprehensible, inconceivable one, the Father, the perfect one, the one who made all things.[4]

In the process, gnostics celebrated—their opponents said they overwhelmingly exaggerated—the greatness of human nature. Humanity itself, in its primordial being, was disclosed to be the "God over all." The philosopher Plotinus, who agreed with his master, Plato, that the universe was divinely created and that nonhuman intelligences, including the stars, share in immortal soul,[5] castigated the gnostics for "thinking very well of themselves, and very ill of the universe."[6]

Although, as the great British scholar Arthur Darby Nock has stated, gnosticism "involves no recoil from society, but a desire to concentrate on inner well being,"[7] the gnostic pursued an essentially solitary path. According to the *Gospel of Thomas*, Jesus praises this solitude: "Blessed are the solitary and the chosen, for you will find the Kingdom. For you are from it, and to it you will return."[8]

This solitude derives from the gnostics' insistence on the primacy of immediate experience. No one else can tell another which way to go, what to do, how to act. The gnostic could not accept on faith what others said, except as a provisional measure, until one found one's own path, "for," as the gnostic teacher Heracleon says, "people at first are led to believe in the Savior through others," but when they become mature "they no longer rely on mere human testimony," but discover instead their own immediate relationship with "the truth itself."[9] Whoever follows secondhand testimony—even testimony of the apostles and the Scriptures—could earn the rebuke Jesus delivered to his disciples when they quoted the prophets to him: "You have ignored the one living in your presence and have spoken (only) of the dead."[10] Only on the basis of immediate experience could one create the poems, vision accounts, myths, and hymns that gnostics prized as proof that one actually has attained *gnosis*.

Compared with that achievement, all others fall away. If "the many"—unenlightened people—believed that they would find fulfillment in family life, sexual relationships, business, politics, ordinary employment or leisure, the gnostic rejected this belief as illusion. Some radicals rejected all transactions involving sexuality or money: they claimed that whoever rejects sexual intercourse and Mammon "shows [that] he is [from] the generation of the [Son of Man]."[11] Others, like the Valentinians,

[145]

married, raised children, worked at ordinary employment, but like devout Buddhists, regarded all these as secondary to the solitary, interior path of *gnosis.*

Orthodox Christianity, on the other hand, articulated a different kind of experience. Orthodox Christians were concerned—far more than gnostics—with their relationships with other people. If gnostics insisted that humanity's original experience of evil involved internal emotional distress, the orthodox dissented. Recalling the story of Adam and Eve, they explained that humanity discovered evil in human violation of the natural order, itself essentially "good." The orthodox interpreted evil (*kakía*) primarily in terms of violence against others (thus giving the moral connotation of the term). They revised the Mosaic code, which prohibits physical violation of others—murder, stealing, adultery—in terms of Jesus' prohibition against even mental and emotional violence—anger, lust, hatred.

Agreeing that human suffering derives from human fault, orthodox Christians affirmed the natural order. Earth's plains, deserts, seas, mountains, stars, and trees form an appropriate home for humanity. As part of that "good" creation, the orthodox recognized the processes of human biology: they tended to trust and affirm sexuality (at least in marriage), procreation, and human development. The orthodox Christian saw Christ not as one who leads souls out of this world into enlightenment, but as "fullness of God" come down into human experience—into *bodily* experience—to sacralize it. Irenaeus declares that Christ

> did not despise or evade any condition of humanity, nor set aside for himself the law which he had appointed for the human race, but sanctified every age . . . He therefore passes through every age, becoming an infant for infants, thus sanctifying infants; a child for children, thus sanctifying those who are at this age . . . a youth for youths . . . and . . . because he was an old man for old people . . . sanctifying at the same time the aged also . . . then, at last, he came onto death itself.[12]

Conclusion

To maintain the consistency of his theory, Irenaeus revised the common tradition that Jesus died in his thirties: lest old age be left unsanctified by Christ's participation, Irenaeus argued that Jesus was more than fifty years old when he died.[13]

But it is not only the story of Christ that makes ordinary life sacred. The orthodox church gradually developed rituals to sanction major events of biological existence: the sharing of food, in the eucharist; sexuality, in marriage; childbirth, in baptism; sickness, in anointment; and death, in funerals. The social arrangements that these events celebrated, in communities, in the family, and in social life, all bore, for the orthodox believer, vitally important ethical responsibilities. The believer heard church leaders constantly warning against incurring sin in the most practical affairs of life: cheating in business, lying to a spouse, tyrannizing children or slaves, ignoring the poor. Even their pagan critics noticed that Christians appealed to the destitute by alleviating two of their major anxieties: Christians provided food for the poor, and they buried the dead.

While the gnostic saw himself as "one out of a thousand, two out of ten thousand,"[14] the orthodox experienced himself as one member of the common human family, and as one member of a universal church. According to Professor Helmut Koester, "the test of orthodoxy is whether it is able to build a *church* rather than a club or school or a sect, or merely a series of concerned religious individuals."[15] Origen, the most brilliant theologian of the third century, expressed, although he was himself brought under suspicion of heresy, the orthodox viewpoint when he declared that God would not have offered a way of salvation accessible only to an intellectual or spiritual elite. What the church teaches, he agreed, must be simple, unanimous, accessible to all. Irenaeus declares that

> as the sun, that creature of God, is one and the same throughout the whole world, so also the preaching of the truth shines everywhere, and enlightens all people who are willing . . . Nor will any one of the rulers in the churches,

[147]

however highly gifted he may be in matters of eloquence,
teach doctrines different from these.[16]

Irenaeus encouraged his community to enjoy the security of
believing that their faith rested upon absolute authority: the
canonically approved Scriptures, the creed, church ritual, and
the clerical hierarchy.

If we go back to the earliest known sources of Christian
tradition—the sayings of Jesus (although scholars disagree on
the question of *which* sayings are genuinely authentic), we can
see how both gnostic and orthodox forms of Christianity could
emerge as variant interpretations of the teaching and significance
of Christ. Those attracted to solitude would note that even the
New Testament gospel of Luke includes Jesus' saying that
whoever "does not hate his own father and mother and wife and
children and brothers and sisters, yes, and even his own life, he
cannot be my disciple."[17] He demanded that those who followed
him must give up everything—family, home, children, ordinary
work, wealth—to join him. And he himself, as prototype, was
a homeless man who rejected his own family, avoided marriage
and family life, a mysterious wanderer who insisted on truth at
all costs, even the cost of his own life. Mark relates that Jesus
concealed his teaching from the masses, and entrusted it only to
the few he considered worthy to receive it.[18]

Yet the New Testament gospels also offer accounts that
lend themselves to a very different interpretation. Jesus blessed
marriage and declared it inviolable;[19] he welcomed the children
who surrounded him;[20] he responded with compassion to the
most common forms of human suffering,[21] such as fever, blind-
ness, paralysis, and mental illness, and wept[22] when he realized
that his people had rejected him. William Blake, noting such
different portraits of Jesus in the New Testament, sided with the
one the gnostics preferred against "the vision of Christ that all
men see":

The vision of Christ that thou dost see
Is my vision's deepest enemy . . .

Thine is the friend of all Mankind,
Mine speaks in parables to the blind:
Thine loves the same world that mine hates,
Thy Heaven doors are my Hell gates ...
Both read the Bible day and night
But thou read'st black where I read white ...
Seeing this False Christ, In fury and passion
I made my Voice heard all over the Nation.[23]

Nietzsche, who detested what he knew as Christianity, nevertheless wrote: "There was only one Christian, and he died on the cross."[24] Dostoevsky, in *The Brothers Karamazov*, attributes to Ivan a vision of the Christ rejected by the church, the Christ who "desired man's free love, that he should follow Thee freely,"[25] choosing the truth of one's own conscience over material well-being, social approval, and religious certainty. Like the author of the *Second Treatise of the Great Seth*, Ivan denounced the orthodox church for seducing people away from "the truth of their freedom."[26]

We can see, then, how conflicts arose in the formation of Christianity between those restless, inquiring people who marked out a solitary path of self-discovery and the institutional framework that gave to the great majority of people religious sanction and ethical direction for their daily lives. Adapting for its own purposes the model of Roman political and military organization, and gaining, in the fourth century, imperial support, orthodox Christianity grew increasingly stable and enduring. Gnostic Christianity proved no match for the orthodox faith, either in terms of orthodoxy's wide popular appeal, what Nock called its "perfect because unconscious correspondence to the needs and aspirations of ordinary humanity,"[27] or in terms of its effective organization. Both have ensured its survival through time. But the process of establishing orthodoxy ruled out every other option. To the impoverishment of Christian tradition, gnosticism, which offered alternatives to what became the main thrust of Christian orthodoxy, was forced outside.

The concerns of gnostic Christians survived only as a suppressed current, like a river driven underground. Such currents resurfaced throughout the Middle Ages in various forms of heresy; then, with the Reformation, Christian tradition again took on new and diverse forms. Mystics like Jacob Boehme, himself accused of heresy, and radical visionaries like George Fox, themselves unfamiliar, in all probability, with gnostic tradition, nevertheless articulated analogous interpretations of religious experience. But the great majority of the movements that emerged from the Reformation—Baptist, Pentecostal, Methodist, Episcopal, Congregational, Presbyterian, Quaker—remained within the basic framework of orthodoxy established in the second century. All regarded the New Testament writings alone as authoritative; most accepted the orthodox creed and retained the Christian sacraments, even when they altered their form and interpretation.

Now that the Nag Hammadi discoveries give us a new perspective on this process, we can understand why certain creative persons throughout the ages, from Valentinus and Heracleon to Blake, Rembrandt, Dostoevsky, Tolstoy, and Nietzsche, found themselves at the edges of orthodoxy. All were fascinated by the figure of Christ—his birth, life, teachings, death, and resurrection: all returned constantly to Christian symbols to express their own experience. And yet they found themselves in revolt against orthodox institutions. An increasing number of people today share their experience. They cannot rest solely on the authority of the Scriptures, the apostles, the church—at least not without inquiring how that authority constituted itself, and what, if anything, gives it legitimacy. All the old questions—the original questions, sharply debated at the beginning of Christianity—are being reopened: How is one to understand the resurrection? What about women's participation in priestly and episcopal office? Who was Christ, and how does he relate to the believer? What are the similarities between Christianity and other world religions?

That I have devoted so much of this discussion to gnosticism does not mean, as the casual reader might assume, that I advocate going back to gnosticism—much less that I "side with it" against orthodox Christianity. As a historian, of course, I find the discoveries at Nag Hammadi enormously exciting, since the evidence they offer opens a new perspective for understanding what fascinates me most—the history of Christianity. But the task of the historian, as I understand it, is not to advocate any side, but to explore the evidence—in this instance, to attempt to discover how Christianity originated. Furthermore, as a person concerned with religious questions, I find that rediscovering the controversies that occupied early Christianity sharpens our awareness of the major issue in the whole debate, then and now: What is the source of religious authority? For the Christian, the question takes more specific form: What is the relation between the authority of one's own experience and that claimed for the Scriptures, the ritual, and the clergy?

When Muḥammed 'Alī smashed that jar filled with papyrus on the cliff near Nag Hammadi and was disappointed not to find gold, he could not have imagined the implications of his accidental find. Had they been discovered 1,000 years earlier, the gnostic texts almost certainly would have been burned for their heresy. But they remained hidden until the twentieth century, when our own cultural experience has given us a new perspective on the issues they raise. Today we read them with different eyes, not merely as "madness and blasphemy" but as Christians in the first centuries experienced them—a powerful alternative to what we know as orthodox Christian tradition. Only now are we beginning to consider the questions with which they confront us.

NOTES

INTRODUCTION

1. J. M. Robinson, Introduction, in *The Nag Hammadi Library* (New York, 1977), 21–22. Hereafter cited as NHL.

2. *Ibid.*, 22.

3. *Gospel of Thomas* 32.10–11, in NHL 118.

4. *Ibid.*, 45.29–33, in NHL 126.

5. *Gospel of Philip* 63.32–64.5, in NHL 138.

6. *Apocryphon of John* 1.2–3, in NHL 99.

7. *Gospel of the Egyptians* 40.12–13, in NHL 195.

8. See discussion by W. Schneemelcher in E. Hennecke, W. Schneemelcher, *New Testament Apocrypha* (transl. from *Neutestamentliche Apocryphen*), (Philadelphia, 1963), I, 97–113. Hereafter cited as NT APOCRYPHA. J. A. Fitzmyer, "The Oxyrhynchus Logoi of Jesus and the Coptic Gospel According to Thomas," in *Essays on the Semitic Background of the New Testament* (Missoula, 1974), 355–433.

9. Robinson, Introduction, in NHL 13–18.

10. Irenaeus, *Libros Quinque Adversus Haereses* 3.11.9. Hereafter cited as AH.

11. M. Malanine, H.-Ch. Puech, G. Quispel, W. Till, R. McL. Wilson, *Evangelium Veritatis* (Zürich and Stuttgart, 1961), Introduction.

12. H. Koester, Introduction to the *Gospel of Thomas*, NHL 117.

13. *Testimony of Truth* 45:23–48:18, in NHL 411–412.

14. *Thunder, Perfect Mind* 13:16–14:15, in NHL 271–272.

15. Irenaeus, AH *Praefatio*.

16. Irenaeus, AH 3.11.9.

17. H. M. Schenke, *Die Herkunft des sogennanten Evangelium Veritatis* (Berlin, 1958; Göttingen, 1959).

Notes

18. Hippolytus, *Refutationis Omnium Haeresium* 1. Hereafter cited as REF.
19. See F. Wisse, "Gnosticism and Early Monasticism in Egypt," in *Gnosis: Festschrift für Hans Jonas* (Göttingen, 1978), 431–440.
20. Theodotus, cited in Clemens Alexandrinus, *Excerpta ex Theodoto* 78.2. Hereafter cited as EXCERPTA.
21. Hippolytus, REF 8.15.1–2. Emphasis added.
22. *Gospel of Thomas* 35.4–7 and 50.28–30, conflated, in NHL 119 and 129.
23. E. Conze, "Buddhism and Gnosis," in *Le Origini dello Gnosticismo: Colloquio di Messina 13–18 Aprile 1966* (Leiden, 1967), 665.
24. Hippolytus, REF 1.24.
25. Conze, "Buddhism and Gnosis," 665–666.
26. One scholar who, even before the Nag Hammadi find, *did* suspect such diversity is W. Bauer, whose book, *Rechtgläubigkeit und Ketzerei im ältesten Christentum*, first appeared in 1934. It was translated and published in English as *Orthodoxy and Heresy in Earliest Christianity* (Philadelphia, 1971).
27. See, for example, Bauer, *Orthodoxy and Heresy*, 111–240.
28. See discussion by H.-Ch. Puech, in NT APOCRYPHA 259 f.
29. *Ibid.*, 250 f.
30. *Ibid.*, 244.
31. H. Jonas, *Journal of Religion* (1961) 262, cited in J. M. Robinson, "The Jung Codex: The Rise and Fall of a Monopoly," in *Religious Studies Review* 3.1 (January 1977), 29.
32. For a more complete account of the events briefly sketched here, see Robinson, "The Jung Codex," 17–30.
33. *La bourse égyptienne* (June 10, 1949), cited in Robinson, "The Jung Codex," 20.
34. G. Quispel, *Jung—een mens voor deze tijd* (Rotterdam, 1975), 85.
35. Robinson, "The Jung Codex," 24 f.
36. E. Pagels, *The Johannine Gospel in Gnostic Exegesis* (Nashville, 1973); *The Gnostic Paul: Gnostic Exegesis of the Pauline Letters* (Philadelphia, 1975).
37. E. Pagels, with H. Koester, "Report on the Dialogue of the Savior" (CG III.5), in R. McL. Wilson, *Nag Hammadi and Gnosis* (Leiden, 1978), 66–74.
38. G. Garitte, *Le Muséon* (1960), 214, cited in Robinson, "The Jung Codex," 29.
39. Tertullian, *Adversus Valentinianos* 7.
40. A. von Harnack, *History of Dogma*, trans. from 3rd German ed. (New York, 1961), I.4, 228.
41. *Ibid.*, 229.
42. A. D. Nock, *Early Gentile Christianity and Its Hellenistic Background*, 2nd ed. (New York, 1964), xvi.

Notes

43. W. Bousset, *Kyrios Christos* (1st ed., Göttingen, 1913; 2nd ed., 1921; English trans., 1970), 245.

44. R. Reitzenstein, *Poimandres: Studien zur griechisch-ägyptischen und frühchristlichen Literatur* (Leipzig, 1904; repr. Darmstadt, 1966), 81. See also *Das iranische Erlösungmysterium* (Leipzig, 1921).

45. M. Friedländer, *Der vorchristliche jüdische Gnosticismus* (Göttingen, 1898; 2nd ed., 1972).

46. H. Jonas, *Gnosis und spätantiker Geist, I: Die mythologische Gnosis* (Göttingen, 1st ed., 1934; 2nd ed., 1964).

47. H. Jonas, *The Gnostic Religion* (Boston, 1st ed., 1958; 2nd ed., 1963).

48. *Ibid.*, 320–340.

49. W. Bauer, *Orthodoxy and Heresy in Earliest Christianity* (trans. from 2nd ed., Philadelphia, 1971), xxii.

50. H. E. W. Turner, *The Pattern of Christian Truth: A Study in the Relations Between Orthodoxy and Heresy in the Early Church* (London, 1954).

51. C. H. Roberts, *Manuscript, Society, and Belief in Early Christian Egypt* (London, 1979).

52. A. Guillaumont, H.-Ch. Puech, G. Quispel, W. Till, Y. 'Abd al Masīḥ, *The Gospel According to Thomas: Coptic Text Established and Translated* (Leiden/New York, 1959).

53. *The Facsimile Edition of the Nag Hammadi Codices*, Codices I–XIII (Leiden, 1972). For discussion, see J. M. Robinson, "The Facsimile Edition of the Nag Hammadi Codices," in *Occasional Papers of the Institute for Antiquity and Christianity*, 4 (Claremont, 1972).

54. C. Colpe, *Die religionsgeschichtliche Schule: Darstellung und Kritik ihres Bildes von gnostischen Erlösermythus* (Göttingen, 1961).

55. R. M. Grant, *Gnosticism and Early Christianity*, 2nd ed. (New York, 1966), 27 ff.

56. G. Quispel, *Gnosis als Weltreligion* (Leiden, 1951).

57. H. Jonas, "Delimitation of the gnostic phenomenon—typological and historical," in *Le Origini dello Gnosticismo* (Leiden, 1967), 90–108.

58. E. R. Dodds, *Pagan and Christian in an Age of Anxiety* (Cambridge, 1965), 69–101.

59. G. G. Scholem, *Jewish Gnosticism, Merkabah Mysticism, and Talmudic Tradition* (New York, 1st ed., 1960; 2nd ed., 1965).

60. A. D. Nock, *Essays on Religion and the Ancient World*, ed. Z. Stewart (Cambridge, 1972), II, "Gnosticism," 940 ff.

61. Cf. A. H. Armstrong, "Gnosis and Greek Philosophy," in *Gnosis: Festschrift für Hans Jonas* (Göttingen, 1978), 87–124.

62. B. Layton, *Treatise on Resurrection: Editing, Translation, Commentary* (Missoula, 1979); "Vision and Revision: A Gnostic View of Resurrection," in *Proceedings: Quebec Colloquium on the Texts of Nag Hammadi* (Quebec, 1979).

Notes

63. See, for example, H. Attridge, "Exegetical Problems in the Tripartite Tractate," prepared for the SBL meetings in New Orleans, 1978, and his edition of Codex I from Nag Hammadi, to be published in *Nag Hammadi Studies* (Leiden, 1980).

64. M. Smith, *Clement of Alexandria and a Secret Gospel of Mark* (Cambridge, 1973); *Jesus the Magician* (San Francisco, 1978).

65. J. M. Robinson, H. Koester, *Trajectories Through Early Christianity* (Philadelphia, 1971): see especially Robinson, "*Logoi Sophon*: On the Gattung of Q," 71–113; Koester, "One Jesus and Four Primitive Gospels," 158–204.

66. M. Tardieu, *Trois mythes gnostiques: Adam, Eros et les animaux dans un écrit de Nag Hammadi* (Paris, 1974).

67. L. Schottroff, *Der Glaubende und die feindliche Welt* (Neukirchener, 1970).

68. P. Perkins, *The Gnostic Dialogue* (New York, 1979).

69. P. Perkins, "Deceiving the Deity: Self-Transcendence and the Numinous in Gnosticism," in *Proceedings of the Tenth Annual Institute for Philosophy and Religion* (Boston, 1981).

70. G. MacRae, "Sleep and Awakening in Gnostic Texts," in *Le Origini dello Gnosticismo*, 496–510.

71. G. MacRae, "The Jewish Background of the Gnostic Sophia Myth," *Novum Testamentum* 12 (1970), 97 ff.

72. For a recent example, see G. MacRae, "Nag Hammadi and the New Testament," in *Gnosis: Festschrift für Hans Jonas*, 144–157.

73. See, for example, B. A. Pearson, "Jewish Haggadic Traditions in the *Testimony of Truth* from Nag Hammadi (CGIX, 3)," in *Ex Orbe Religionum: Studia Geo Widengren* (Leiden, 1972), 457–470; "Biblical Exegesis in Gnostic Literature," in *Armenian and Biblical Studies*, ed. M. E. Stone (Jerusalem, 1975), 70–80; "The Figure of Melchizedek," in *Proceedings of the XIIth International Congress of the International Association for the History of Religions* (Leiden, 1975), 200–208.

74. D. M. Scholer, *Nag Hammadi Bibliography* (Leiden, 1971).

75. *Apocalypse of Peter* 76.27–30, in NHL 342. In quotations from this text, I am following the translations of J. Brashler, *The Coptic Apocalypse of Peter: A Genre Analysis and Interpretation* (Claremont, 1977).

CHAPTER ONE

For a more technical discussion of this topic, scholars are advised to consult E. Pagels, "Visions, Appearances, and Apostolic Authority: Gnostic and Orthodox Traditions," in *Gnosis: Festschrift für Hans Jonas*, ed. B. Aland (Göttingen, 1978), 415–430.

Notes

1. K. Stendahl, *Immortality and Resurrection* (New York, 1968).
2. Luke 24:36–43.
3. Acts 2:22–36.
4. *Ibid.*, 10:40–41.
5. Tertullian, *De Resurrectione Carnis* 2.
6. Tertullian, *De Carne Christi* 5.
7. *Ibid.*
8. John 20:27.
9. Mark 16:12; Luke 24:13–32.
10. Luke 24:31.
11. John 20:11–17.
12. Acts 9:3–4.
13. *Ibid.*, 9:7.
14. *Ibid.*, 22:9.
15. I. Corinthians 15:50.
16. *Ibid.*, 15:51–53.
17. Mark 10:42–44.
18. Luke 24:34.
19. Matthew 16:13–19.
20. John 21:15–19.
21. H. von Campenhausen, *Ecclesiastical Authority and Spiritual Power* (London, 1969), trans. by J. A. Baker (original title: *Kirchliches Amt und geistliche Vollmacht*, Tübingen, 1953), 17 (see discussion in Ch. 1).
22. Mark 16:9; John 20:11–17.
23. Matthew 28:16–20; Luke 24:36–49; John 20:19–23.
24. Matthew 28:18.
25. Acts 1:15–20.
26. *Ibid.*, 1:22. Emphasis added.
27. *Ibid.*, 1:26.
28. *Ibid.*, 1:6–11.
29. *Ibid.*, 7:56.
30. Acts 9:1–6.
31. *Ibid.*, 22:17–18; cf. also Acts 18:9–10.
32. See J. Lindblom, *Gesichte und Offenbarungen: Vorstellungen von göttlichen Weisungen und übernatürlichen Erscheinungen im ältesten Christentum* (Lund, 1968), 32–113.
33. See K. Holl, *Der Kirchenbegriff des Paulus in seinem Verhältnis zu dem der Urgemeinde*, in *Gesammelte Aufsätze zur Kirchengeschichte* (Tübingen, 1921), II, 50–51.
34. G. Blum, *Tradition und Sukzession: Studium zum Normbegriff des Apostolischen von Paulus bis Irenaeus* (Berlin, 1963), 48.
35. Campenhausen, *Ecclesiastical Authority and Spiritual Power*, 14–24. For discussion, see E. Pagels, "Visions, Appearances, and Apostolic Authority," 415–430.

36. Origen, *Commentarium in I Corinthians*, in *Journal of Theological Studies* 10 (1909), 46–47.

37. Tertullian, *De Resurrectione Carnis*, 19–27.

38. Irenaeus, AH 1.30.13.

39. I Corinthians 15:8.

40. Mark 16:9.

41. John 20:11–19.

42. *Gospel of Mary* 10.17–21, in NHL 472.

43. *Apocalypse of Peter* 83.8–10, in NHL 344. For discussion of Peter in gnostic traditions, see P. Perkins, "Peter in Gnostic Revelations," in *Proceedings of SBL: 1974 Seminar Papers II* (Washington, 1974), 1–13.

44. *Treatise on Resurrection* 48.10–16, in NHL 52–53. See M. L. Peel, *The Epistle to Rheginos; A Valentinian Letter on the Resurrection: Introduction, Translation, Analysis, and Exposition* (London/Philadelphia 1969); B. Layton, *The Gnostic Treatise on Resurrection from Nag Hammadi. Edited, with Translation and Commentary* (Missoula, 1979). The translation I cite follows that of Layton, as noted in the Acknowledgments.

45. *Treatise on Resurrection* 48.34–38, in NHL 53.

46. *Ibid.*, 47.18–49.24, in NHL 53.

47. *Gospel of Philip* 73.1–3, in NHL 144.

48. *Ibid.*, 57.19–20, in NHL 135.

49. Cf. H. Koester, "One Jesus and Four Primitive Gospels," in J. M. Robinson and H. Koester, *Trajectories through Early Christianity* (Philadelphia, 1971), 158–204, and Robinson, "The Johannine Trajectory," *ibid.*, 232–268.

50. Mark 16:9–20.

51. *Gospel of Mary* 9.14–18, in NHL 472.

52. *Ibid.*, 10.4–5, in NHL 472.

53. *Ibid.*, 17.8–15, in NHL 473.

54. *Ibid.*, 18.1–12, in NHL 473.

55. The author of the *Gospel of Mary* may have noted that neither Mark nor John specifies that the resurrected Jesus appeared *physically* to Mary. Mark's account, which adds that Jesus later appeared "in another form," could be taken to suggest that he was a disembodied presence who took on various forms in order to become visible. John's account relates that Jesus warned Mary not to touch him—in contrast to the stories that say he insisted on the disciples' touching him to prove that he was "not a ghost."

56. Irenaeus, AH 3.2.1–3.3.1. See also M. Smith, *Clement of Alexandria and a Secret Gospel of Mark* (Cambridge, 1973), 197–278.

57. *Ibid.*, 3.4.1–2.

58. Mark 4:11.

59. Matthew 13:11.

60. II Corinthians 12:2–4.

61. I Corinthians 2:6.

62. R. Bultmann, *Theology of the New Testament*, trans. by K. Grobel (London, 1965), I, 327; U. Wilckens, *Weisheit und Torheit* (Tübingen, 1959), 44 f., 214–224.

63. R. Scroggs, "Paul: Σόφος and πνευμάτικος," *New Testament Studies* 14, 33–55. See also E. Pagels, *The Gnostic Paul* (Philadelphia, 1975), 1–10; 55–58; 157–164.

64. *Apocryphon of John* 1.30–2.7, in NHL 99.

65. *Ibid.*, 2.9–18, in NHL 99.

66. *Letter of Peter to Philip* 134.10–18, in NHL 395. For analysis, see M. Meyer, *The Letter of Peter to Philip NHL VIII, 2: Text, Translation, and Commentary* (Claremont, 1979).

67. *Sophia Jesu Christi* 91.8–13, in NHL 207–208.

68. For discussion, see H.-C. Puech, "Gnostic Gospels and Related Documents," in *New Testament Apocrypha* I. 231–362.

69. *Gospel of Philip* 57.28–35, in NHL 135.

70. Clemens Alexandrinus, EXCERPTA 23.4.

71. Irenaeus, AH 3.11.9.

72. *Book of Thomas the Contender* 138.7–18, in NHL 189.

73. Irenaeus, AH 1.18.1.

74. *Acts of John* 94–96, in *New Testament Apocrypha* II. 227–232. For brief discussion, see E. Pagels, "To the Universe Belongs the Dancer," in *Parabola* IV.2 (1979), 7–9.

75. Irenaeus, AH 2.15.3.

76. *Ibid.*, 2.13.3–10. Emphasis added.

77. Heracleon, Frag. 39, in Origen, *Commentarium in Johannes*. Hereafter cited as COMM. JO.

78. Hippolytus, REF 6.42.

79. Irenaeus, AH 1.14.1.

80. *Ibid.*, 1.14.3.

81. *Ibid.*, 1.13.3–4.

82. *Ibid.*, 3.4.1.

83. *Ibid.*, 1.13.6.

84. *Ibid.*, 3.2.2.

85. Ptolemy, *Epistula ad Floram* 7.9; for discussion, see Campenhausen, *Ecclesiastical Authority and Spiritual Power*, 158–161.

86. Irenaeus, AH 1.30.13.

87. *Dialogue of the Savior* 139.12–13, in NHL 235.

88. *Apocalypse of Peter* 72.10–28, in NHL 340–341.

89. *Apocryphon of James* 2.8–15, in NHL 30.

90. Tertullian, *De Praescriptione Haereticorum* 42. Hereafter cited as DE PRAESCR.

91. *Ibid.*, 37.

92. Irenaeus, AH 1.10.2.

93. *Ibid.*, 3.4.1.

94. *Ibid.*, 3.3.2.

95. *Apocalypse of Peter* 74.16–21, in NHL 341. Cf. Brashler, *The Coptic Apocalypse of Peter*; Perkins, "Peter in Gnostic Revelations."

96. *Apocalypse of Peter* 79.24–30, in NHL 343.

97. *Ibid.*, 76.27–34, in NHL 342.

98. *Ibid.*, 78.31–79.10, in NHL 343.

99. For discussion, see E. Pagels, "The Demiurge and his Archons: A Gnostic View of the Bishop and Presbyters?" in *Harvard Theological Review* 69.3–4 (1976), 301–324.

100. Tertullian, *De Carne Christi* 5.

101. *Gospel of Thomas*, 38.33–39.2, in NHL 121.

102. Cf. E. Leach, *Melchisedek and the Emperor: Icons of Subversion and Orthodoxy*, in *Proceedings of the Royal Anthropological Institute of Great Britain and Ireland for 1972* (London, 1973), 1 ff.

CHAPTER TWO

For a more technical discussion of this subject, see E. Pagels, "The Demiurge and his Archons: A Gnostic View of the Bishop and Presbyters?" in *Harvard Theological Review* 69.3–4 (1976), 301–324.

1. Cf. N. A. Dahl, "The Gnostic Response: The Ignorant Creator," documentation prepared for the Nag Hammadi Section of the Society of Biblical Literature Annual Meeting, 1976.

2. *Hypostasis of the Archons* 86.27–94.26, in NHL 153–158. Note that the citation is conflated from two separate variants of the story in 86.27–87.4 and 94.19–26; a third occurs in the same text at 94.34–95.13. Cf. B. Layton, "The Hypostasis of the Archons," *Harvard Theological Review* 67 (1974), 351 ff.

3. *On the Origin of the World* 103.9–20, in NHL 165. For analysis of the texts, see F. L. Fallon, *The Sabaoth Accounts in "The Nature of the Archons" (CG 11,4) and "On the Origin of the World" (CG 11,5): An Analysis* (Cambridge, 1974).

4. *Apocryphon of John* 11.18–13.13, in NHL 105–106.

5. *Testimony of Truth* 45.24–46.11, in NHL 411.

6. *Ibid.*, 47.7–30, in NHL 412.

7. See excellent discussion by B. A. Pearson, "Jewish Haggadic Traditions in the Testimony of Truth from Nag Hammadi, CG IX, 3," in *Ex Orbe Religionum: Studia Geo Widengren oblata* (Leiden, 1972), 458–470.

8. *On the Origin of the World* 115.31–116.8, in NHL 172.

9. *Hypostasis of the Archons* 89.11–91.1, in NHL 154–155.

10. *Tripartite Tractate* 51.24–52.6, in NHL 55.

11. *A Valentinian Exposition* 22.19–23, in NHL 436.

12. *Interpretation of Knowledge* 9.29, in NHL 430.

13. Irenaeus, AH 4.33.3.

14. *Ibid.*, 3.16.6.

15. *Ibid.*, 3.16.8.

16. *Ibid., Praefatio* 2.

17. *Ibid.*, 4.33.3; 3.16.8.

18. For discussion and references, see Pagels, "The Demiurge and his Archons."

19. Irenaeus, AH 1.11.1.

20. *Ibid.*, 1.1.1; cf. *Tripartite Tractate* 51.1 ff., in NHL 55 ff.

21. Heracleon, Frag. 22, in Origen, COMM. JO. 13.19.

22. *Ibid.*, Frag. 24, in Origen, COMM. JO. 13.25.

23. *Gospel of Philip* 53.24–34, in NHL 132–133.

24. Irenaeus, AH 3.15.2. Emphasis added.

25. Clemens Romanus, *I Clement* 3.3.

26. *Ibid.*, 1.1.

27. *Ibid.*, 14.19–20; 60.

28. *Ibid.*, 60.4–61.2; 63.1–2.

29. *Ibid.*, 63.1.

30. *Ibid.*, 41.3.

31. *Ibid.*, 41.1.

32. See, for example, Campenhausen, *Ecclesiastical Authority and Spiritual Power*, 86–87: "Dogmatic issues are nowhere mentioned. We can no longer discern the background and the real point of the quarrel."

33. So says H. Beyschlag, *Clemens Romanus und der Frühkatholizismus* (Tübingen, 1966), 339–353.

34. Ignatius, *Magnesians* 6.1; *Trallians* 3.1; *Ephesians* 5.3.

35. *Magnesians* 6.1–7.2; *Trallians* 3.1; *Smyrneans* 8.1–2. For citations and discussion, see Pagels, "The Demiurge and his Archons," 306–307.

36. *Trallians* 3.1; *Smyrneans* 8.2.

37. See, for example, Campenhausen, *Ecclesiastical Authority and Spiritual Power*, 84–106.

38. Tertullian, *Adversus Valentinianos* 4.

39. Clemens Alexandrinus, *Stromata* 7.7.

40. Irenaeus, AH 3.2.1–3.1.

41. *Ibid., Praefatio* 2; 3.15.1–2.

42. Clemens Alexandrinus, *Stromata* 4.89.6–90.1.

43. Cf. Plato, *Timaeus* 41. For discussion, see G. Quispel, "The Origins of the Gnostic Demiurge," in *Kyriakon: Festschrift Johannes Quasten* (Münster, 1970), 252–271.

44. Heracleon, Frag. 40, in Origen, COMM. JO. 13.60.

45. *Lord*: Irenaeus, AH 4.1–5.

46. *commander*: Ibid., 1.7.4.

47. *judge*: Heracleon, Frag. 48, in Origen, COMM. JO. 20.38.

48. Irenaeus, AH 3.12.6–12.

49. *Ibid.*, 1.21.1–4.
50. *Ibid.*, 1.13.6.
51. *Ibid.*, 1.21.5.
52. *Ibid.*, 3.15.2.
53. *Ibid.*, 1.7.4.
54. *Ibid.*, 1.13.6.
55. *Ibid.*, 3.15.2.
56. Tertullian, *Adversus Valentinianos* 4.
57. Irenaeus, AH 3.15.2.
58. *Ibid.*, 3.3.2.
59. *Ibid.*, 3.15.2.
60. *Ibid.*, 1.21.1–2.
61. For a detailed discussion of this process, see Campenhausen, *Ecclesiastical Authority and Spiritual Power*, 76 ff.
62. *Apocalypse of Peter* 79.22–30, in NHL 343.
63. *Tripartite Tractate* 69.7–10, in NHL 64; 70.21–29, in NHL 65; 72.16–19, in NHL 66.
64. *Ibid.*, 79.20–32, in NHL 69.
65. Irenaeus, AH 1.13.1–6.
66. *Ibid.*, 1.13.3
67. *Ibid.*, 1.13.4; for technical discussion of the lot (*kleros*), see Pagels, "The Demiurge and his Archons," 316–318.
Irenaeus tries to deny this: AH 1.13.4.
Such use of lots had precedent both in ancient Israel, where God was thought to express His choice through the casting of lots, and also among the apostles themselves, who selected by lot the twelfth apostle to replace Judas Iscariot (Acts 1:17–20). Apparently the followers of Valentinus intended to follow their example.
68. Tertullian, DE PRAESCR. 41. Emphasis added.
69. *Ibid.*, 41.
70. *Ibid.*, 41.
71. Irenaeus, AH 1.13.1.
72. *Ibid.*, 1.6.2–3.
73. *Ibid.*, Quotation conflated from 3.15.2 and 2.16.4.
74. *Ibid.*, 3.15.2.
75. *Ibid.*, 3.25.1.
76. *Ibid.*, 5.26.1.
77. Irenaeus, *Ad Florinum*, in Eusebius, *Historia ecclesiae* 5.20.4–8.
78. Irenaeus, AH 4.26.3. Emphasis added.
79. *Ibid.*, 4.26.2.
80. *Ibid.*, 4.26.2.
81. *Ibid.*, 1.27.4.
82. *Ibid.*, 5.31.1.
83. *Ibid.*, 5.35.2.

Notes

CHAPTER THREE

1. Where the God of Israel is characterized as husband and lover in the Old Testament, his spouse is described as the community of Israel (e.g., Isaiah 50:1; 54:1–8; Jeremiah 2:2–3; 20–25; 3:1–20; Hosea 1–4, 14) or as the land of Israel (Isaiah 62:1–5).

2. One may note several exceptions to this rule: Deuteronomy 32:11; Hosea 11:1; Isaiah 66:12 ff.; Numbers 11:12.

3. Formerly, as Professor Morton Smith reminds me, theologians often used the masculinity of God to justify, by analogy, the roles of men as rulers of their societies and households (he cites, for example, Milton's *Paradise Lost* IV.296 ff., 635 ff.).

4. *Gospel of Thomas* 51.19–26, in NHL 130.

5. Hippolytus, REF 5.6.

6. Irenaeus, AH 1.11.1.

7. *Ibid.*, 1.13.6.

8. *Ibid.*, 1.13.2.

9. *Ibid.*, 1.13.2.

10. *Ibid.*, 1.14.1.

11. Hippolytus, REF 6. 18.

12. *Ibid.*, 6.17.

13. Irenaeus, AH 1.11.5; Hippolytus, REF 6.29.

14. *Apocryphon of John* 1.31–2.9, in NHL 99.

15. *Ibid.*, 2.9–14, in NHL 99.

16. *Ibid.*, 4.34–5.7, in NHL 101.

17. *Gospel to the Hebrews*, cited in Origen, COMM. JO. 2.12.

18. *Gospel of Thomas* 49.32–50.1, in NHL 128–129.

19. *Gospel of Philip* 52.24, in NHL 132.

20. *Ibid.*, 59.35–60.1, in NHL 136.

21. Hippolytus, REF 6.14.

22. *Ibid.*, 5.19.

23. Irenaeus, AH 1.14.7–8.

24. *Gospel of Philip* 71.3–5, in NHL 143.

25. *Ibid.*, 71.16–19, in NHL 143.

26. *Ibid.*, 55.25–26, in NHL 134.

27. Hippolytus, REF 6.38.

28. *Apocalypse of Adam* 81.2–9, in NHL 262. See note #42 for references.

29. Irenaeus, AH 1.2.2–3.

30. *Ibid.*, 1.4.1.–1.5.4.

31. *Ibid.*, 1.5.1–3. For discussion of the figure of Sophia, see the excellent articles of G. C. Stead, "The Valentinian Myth of Sophia," in *Journal of Theological Studies* 20 (1969), 75–104; and G. W. MacRae,

"The Jewish Background of the Gnostic Sophia Myth," in *Novum Testamentum* 12.

32. Clemens Alexandrinus, EXCERPTA 47.1.

33. Irenaeus, AH 1.13.1–6.

34. *Ibid.*, 1.30.9.

35. *Ibid.*, 1.30.10.

36. *Trimorphic Protennoia* 35.1–24, in NHL 461–462.

37. *Ibid.*, 36.12–16, in NHL 462.

38. *Ibid.*, 42.4–26, in NHL 465–466.

39. *Ibid.*, 45.2–10, in NHL 467.

40. *Thunder, Perfect Mind* 13.16–16.25, in NHL 271–274.

41. Hippolytus, REF 6.18.

42. *Genesis Rabba* 8.1, cited in an excellent discussion of androgyny by W. A. Meeks, "The Image of the Androgyne: Some Uses of a Symbol in Earliest Christianity," in *History of Religions* 13.3 (February 1974), 165–208. For a discussion of androgyny in gnostic sources, see Pagels, "The Gnostic Vision," in *Parabola* 3.4 (November 1978), 6–9.

43. Irenaeus, AH 1.18.2.

44. Clemens Alexandrinus, EXERPTA 21.1.

45. Hippolytus, REF 6.33.

46. Irenaeus, AH 1.5.4; Hippolytus, REF 6.33.

47. *Ibid.*, 1.29.4.

48. *Apocryphon of John* 13.8–14, in NHL 106.

49. Irenaeus, AH 1.30.6.

Note the collection of passages cited by N. A. Dahl in "The Gnostic Response: The Ignorant Creator," prepared for the Nag Hammadi Section of the Society of Biblical Literature Annual Meeting, 1976.

50. *Hypostasis of the Archons* 94.21–95.7, in NHL 158.

51. Hippolytus, REF 6.32.

52. Irenaeus, AH 1.13.5.

53. *Ibid.*, 1.13.3.

54. *Ibid.*, 1.13.4.

55. *Ibid.*, 1.13.3.

56. Hippolytus, REF 6.35; Irenaeus, AH 1.13.1–2.

57. Tertullian, DE PRAESCR. 41.

58. Tertullian, *De Baptismo* 1.

59. Tertullian, *De Virginibus Velandis* 9. Emphasis added.

60. Irenaeus, AH 1.25.6.

61. This general observation is not, however, universally applicable. At least two circles where women acted on an equal basis with men—the Marcionites and the Montanists—retained a traditional doctrine of God. I know of no evidence to suggest that they included feminine imagery in their theological formulations. For discussion and references, see J. Leipoldt, *Die Frau in der antiken Welt und im Urchristentum* (Leipzig,

1955), 187 ff.; E. S. Fiorenza, "Word, Spirit, and Power: Women in Early Christian Communities," in *Women of Spirit*, ed. R. Reuther and E. McLaughlin (New York, 1979), 39 ff.

62. Luke 10:38–42.

Cf. Romans 16:1–2; Colossians 4:15; Acts 2:25; 21:9; Romans 16:6; 16:12; Philippians 4:2–3.

63. See W. Meeks, "The Image of the Androgyne," 180 f. Most scholars agree with Meeks that in Galatians 3:28, Paul quotes a saying that itself belongs to pre-Pauline tradition.

64. Romans 16:7.

This was first pointed out to me by Cyril C. Richardson, and confirmed by recent research of B. Brooten, "Junia . . . Outstanding Among the Apostles," in *Women Priests*, ed. L. and A. Swidler (New York, 1977), 141–144.

65. I Corinthians 11:7–9.

For discussion of I Corinthians 11:7–9, see R. Scroggs, "Paul and the Eschatological Woman," in *Journal of the American Academy of Religion* 40 (1972), 283–303, and the critique by Pagels, "Paul and Women: A Response to Recent Discussion," in *Journal of the American Academy of Religion* 42 (1974), 538–549. Also see references in Fiorenza, "Word, Spirit, and Power," 62, n. 24 and 25.

66. See Leipoldt, *Die Frau*; also C. Schneider, *Kulturgeschichte des Hellenismus* (Munich, 1967), I, 78 ff.; S. A. Pomeroy, *Goddesses, Whores, Wives, and Slaves* (New York, 1975).

67. Cf. C. Vatin, *Recherches sur le mariage et la condition de la femme mariée à l'époque hellénistique* (Paris, 1970).

68. J. Carcopino, *Daily Life in Ancient Rome*, trans. by E. O. Lorimer (New Haven, 1951), 95–100.

69. *Ibid.*, 90–95.

70. L. Swidler, "Greco-Roman Feminism and the Reception of the Gospel," in *Traditio—Krisis—Renovatio*, ed. B. Jaspert (Marburg, 1976), 41–55; see also J. Balsdon, *Roman Women, Their History and Habits* (London, 1962); L. Friedländer, *Roman Life and Manners Under the Early Empire* (Oxford, 1928); B. Förtsch, *Die politische Rolle der Frau in der römischen Republik* (Stuttgart, 1935). On women in Christian communities, see Fiorenza, "Word, Spirit, and Power"; R. Gryson, *The Ministry of Women in the Early Church* (Minnesota, 1976); K. Thraede, "Frau," *Reallexikon für Antike und Christentum* VIII (Stuttgart, 1973), 197–269.

71. Leipoldt, *Die Frau*, 72 ff.; R. H. Kennet, *Ancient Hebrew Social Life and Custom* (London, 1933); G. F. Moore, *Judaism in the First Centuries of the Christian Era* (Cambridge, 1932).

72. I Timothy 2:11–12.

73. Ephesians 5:24; Colossians 3:18.

Notes

74. *I Clement* 1.3.

75. Leipoldt, *Die Frau,* 192; *Hippolytus of Rome,* 43.1, ed. Paul de Lagarder (*Aegyptiaca,* 1883), 253.

76. Leipoldt, *Die Frau,* 193. Emphasis added.

77. *Gospel of Philip* 63.32–64.5, in NHL 138.

78. *Dialogue of the Savior* 139.12–13, in NHL 235.

79. *Gospel of Mary* 17.18–18.15, in NHL 473.

80. *Pistis Sophia* 36.71.

81. I Timothy 3:1–7; Titus 1:5–9.

82. *Apostolic Tradition* 18.3.

83. *Book of Thomas the Contender* 144.8–10, in NHL 193.

84. *Paraphrase of Shem* 27.2–6; in NHL 320.

85. *Dialogue of the Savior* 144.16–20, in NHL 237.

86. *Ibid.,* 139.12–13, in NHL 235.

87. *Gospel of Thomas* 51.23–26, in NHL 130.

88. *Ibid.,* 37.20–35, in NHL 121; 43.25–35, in NHL 124–125.

89. *Gospel of Mary* 9.20, in NHL 472. Emphasis added.

90. Clemens Alexandrinus, *Paidagogos* 1.6.

91. *Ibid.,* 1.4.

92. *Ibid.,* 1.19.

93. Tertullian, DE VIRG. VEL. 9.

CHAPTER FOUR

For a more technical discussion of this topic, see E. Pagels, "Gnostic and Orthodox Views of Christ's Passion: Paradigms for the Christian's Response to Persecution?" in *The Rediscovery of Gnosticism,* ed. B. Layton (Leiden, 1979), I.

1. Tacitus, *Annals* 15.44.2–8. Emphasis added.

2. Josephus, *Antiquities of the Jews* 18.63.

3. Mark 14:43–50.

4. *Ibid.,* 15:1–15.

5. *Ibid.,* 15:37.

6. Luke 23:34–46; John 19:17–30.

7. Mark 15:10.

8. John 11:45–53.

9. Josephus, *The Jewish War* 2.223–233.

10. John 11:47–48.

11. *Ibid.,* 11:49–50.

12. *Apocalypse of Peter* 81.4–24, in NHL 344. Note, again, use of translation by J. Brashler, *The Coptic Apocalypse of Peter.*

13. *Second Treatise of the Great Seth* 56.6–19 in NHL 332.

14. *Acts of John* 88, in NT APOCRYPHA II, 225.

15. *Ibid.*, 89, in NT APOCRYPHA II, 225.

16. *Ibid.*, 93, in NT APOCRYPHA II, 227.

17. *Ibid.*, 94, in NT APOCRYPHA II, 227.

18. *Ibid.*, 95.16–96.42, in NT APOCRYPHA II, 229–231. For discussion, see E. Pagels, "To the Universe Belongs the Dancer," in *Parabola* IV.2 (1979), 7–9.

19. *Ibid.*, 97, in NT APOCRYPHA II, 232.

20. *Ibid.*, 97, in NT APOCRYPHA II, 232.

21. *Ibid.*, 101, in NT APOCRYPHA II, 234.

22. *Treatise on Resurrection* 44.13–45.29, in NHL 51; for discussion, see Pagels, "Gnostic and Orthodox Views of Christ's Passion," also K. F. Tröger, *Die Passion Jesu Christi in der Gnosis nach den Schriften von Nag Hammadi* (Berlin, 1978).

23. Suetonius, *Life of Nero* 6.16.

24. Tacitus, *Annals* 15.44–2–8.

25. See the discussion by R. MacMullen, *Enemies of the Roman Order: Treason, Unrest, and Alienation in the Empire* (Cambridge, 1966).

26. M. Smith, *Jesus the Magician* (San Francisco, 1978).

27. *Ibid.*; especially 81–139.

28. For a fuller discussion, see W. H. C. Frend, *Martyrdom and Persecution in the Early Church* (Oxford, 1965; New York, 1967); Frend, "The Gnostic Sects and the Roman Empire," in *Journal of Ecclesiastical History*, Vol. V (1954), 25–37.

29. Pliny, *Epistles* 10.96. Emphasis added.

30. *Ibid.*, 10.97. Emphasis added.

31. Justin Martyr, I *Apology* 1.

32. Justin, II *Apology* 2.

33. *Ibid.*, *Apology* 3.

34. "The Martyrdom of Saints Justin, Chariton, Charito, Euelpistis, Hierax, Paeon, Liberian, and Their Community," Recension A, 3, in *The Acts of the Christian Martyrs*, ed. H. Mursurillo (Oxford, 1972), 47–53. Hereafter cited as CHRISTIAN MARTYRS.

35. *Ibid.*, Recension B, 5, in CHRISTIAN MARTYRS, 53.

36. *Loc. cit.*

37. "Martyrdom of Saint Polycarp" 9–10, in CHRISTIAN MARTYRS, 9–11. Emphasis added.

38. "Acts of the Scillitan Martyrs" 1–3, in CHRISTIAN MARTYRS, 86–87.

39. *Ibid.*, 14, in CHRISTIAN MARTYRS, 88–89.

40. Tertullian contemptuously cites their arguments in *Scorpiace* 1.

41. Ignatius, *Romans* 6.3.

42. *Ibid.*, 4.1–5.3.

43. Ignatius, *Trallians* 9.1.

44. *Ibid.*, 10.1. Emphasis added.

45. Ignatius, *Smyrneans* 5.1–2.

46. Justin, II *Apology* 12.

47. Justin, *Dialogue with Trypho* 110.4.
48. Justin, I *Apology* 13.
49. Justin, II *Apology* 15.
50. Frend, *Martyrdom and Persecution in the Early Church*, 5–6.
51. "Martyrs of Lyons" 9, in CHRISTIAN MARTYRS, 64–65.
52. *Ibid.*, 15, in CHRISTIAN MARTYRS, 66–67.
53. *Ibid.*, 18–56, in CHRISTIAN MARTYRS, 67–81.
54. Irenaeus, AH 3.18.5.
55. *Ibid.*, 3.16.9–3.18.4. Emphasis added.
56. *Ibid.*, 3.18.5. Emphasis added.
57. Tertullian, *Apology* 15.
58. Tertullian, *De Anima* 55.
59. Tertullian, *Scorpiace* 1. Emphasis added.
60. *Ibid.*, 1, 5, 7. Emphasis added.
61. Hippolytus, REF 10.33. Emphasis added.
62. Irenaeus, AH 4.33.9. Emphasis added.
63. *Apocryphon of James* 4.37–6.18, in NHL 31–32. Emphasis added. On the figure of James, see S. K. Brown, *James: A Religio-Historical Study of the Relations between Jewish, Gnostic, and Catholic Christianity in the Early Period through an Investigation of the Traditions about James the Lord's Brother* (Providence, 1972).
64. *Apocryphon of James*, 6.19–20, in NHL 32.
65. 2 *Apocalypse of James* 47.24–25, in NHL 250.
66. *Ibid.*, 48.8–9, in NHL 250.
67. *Ibid.*, 61.9–62.12, in NHL 254–255.
68. *Testimony of Truth* 31.22–32.8, in NHL 407.
69. *Ibid.*, 33.25–34.26, in NHL 408.
70. "Martyrdom of Polycarp" 2, in CHRISTIAN MARTYRS, 4–5.
71. Tertullian, *Apology* 50.
72. "Martyrdom of Saint Justin" (Recension C) 4, in CHRISTIAN MARTYRS, 58–59.
73. *Testimony of Truth* 30.18–20; 32.22–33.11, in NHL 408.
74. *Apocalypse of Peter* 72.5–9, in NHL 340.
75. *Ibid.*, 73.23–24, in NHL 341.
76. *Ibid.*, 74.1–3, in NHL 341.
77. *Ibid.*, 74.5–15, in NHL 341.
78. *Ibid.*, 79.11–21, in NHL 343.
79. *Ibid.*, 78.1–2, in NHL 342.
80. *Ibid.*, 80.5–6, in NHL 343.
81. *Ibid.*, 78.31–79.2, in NHL 343.
82. *Ibid.*, 81.15–24, in NHL 344.
83. *Ibid.*, 83.12–15, in NHL 344.
84. *Gospel of Truth* 18.24–20.6, in NHL 38–39.
85. *Ibid.*, 18.24–31, in NHL 38.
86. *Ibid.*, 20.10–32, in NHL 39.

87. *Tripartite Tractate* 113.32–34, in NHL 86–87.
88. *Ibid.*, 114.33–115.11, in NHL 87.
89. *Ibid.*, 113.35–38, in NHL 87.
90. *Gospel of Truth* 23.33–24.9, in NHL 41.
91. *Interpretation of the Knowledge* 10.27–30, in NHL 430.
92. Irenaeus, AH 3.18.5.
93. Luke 12:8–12.
94. Clemens Alexandrinus, *Stromata* 4.71 ff.
95. *Ibid.*, 4.33.7.
96. *Loc. cit.*
97. Tacitus, *Annals* 15.44.2–8.
98. "Martyrs of Lyons" 57–60, in CHRISTIAN MARTYRS, 80–81.
99. Justin, *Dialogue with Trypho* 110.
100. Tertullian, *Ad Scapulam* 5.
101. Tertullian, *Apology* 50.

CHAPTER FIVE

1. For excellent discussions of gnostic polemic against orthodox Christianity, see K. Koschorke, *Die Polemik der Gnostiker gegen das kirchliche Christentum* (Leiden, 1978); P. Perkins, "The Gnostic Revelation: Dialogue as Religious Polemic," in W. Haase, *Aufstieg und Niedergang der römischer Welt* II.22 (Berlin/New York, 1980); also P. Perkins, *The Gnostic Dialogue* (New York, 1980).
2. *Second Treatise of the Great Seth* 59.22–29, in NHL 333–334. For analysis, see J. A. Gibbons, *A Commentary on "The Second Logos of the Great Seth"* (New Haven, 1972).
3. *Ibid.*, 60.21–25, in NHL 334.
4. *Ibid.*, 53.27–33, in NHL 331.
5. *Ibid.*, 61.20, in NHL 334.
6. *Apocalypse of Peter* 74.16–22, in NHL 341.
7. *Ibid.*, 74.24–77.28, in NHL 341–342.
8. *Ibid.*, 76.27–34, in NHL 342.
9. *Ibid.*, 79.28–29, in NHL 343.
10. *Testimony of Truth* 31.24–32.2, in NHL 407.
11. *Authoritative Teaching* 26.20–21, in NHL 280.
12. *Ibid.*, 32.18–19, in NHL 282.
13. *Gospel of Philip* 64.23–24, in NHL 139.
14. Ignatius, *Smyrneans* 8.1–2.
15. *Ibid.*, 8.2.
16. *Trallians* 3.1.
17. Irenaeus, AH 4.33.8.
18. *Loc. cit.*

19. *Ibid.*, 3.4.1.
20. *Ibid.*, 3.15.2.
21. *Ibid.*, 5, *Praefatio.*
22. *Apocalypse of Peter* 70.24–71.4, in NHL 340.
23. *Ibid.*, 71.20–21, in NHL 340.
24. *Ibid.*, 79.1–4, in NHL 343.
25. *Second Treatise of the Great Seth* 67.32–68.9, in NHL 337.
26. *Ibid.*, 67.2–5, in NHL 336.
27. *Ibid.*, 70.9, in NHL 338.
28. C. Andresen, *Die Kirche der alten Christenheit* (Stuttgart, 1971), 100 ff.; see also Jonas, *Gnosis und spätantiker Geist* (Göttingen, 1964), "Solipcismus und Brüderethik," I.171–172.
29. Hippolytus, REF 9.7.
30. *Ibid.*, 9.12.
31. Tertullian, *Adversus Valentinianos* 4.
32. Tertullian, DE PRAESCR. 13.
33. *Ibid.*, 38.
34. *Ibid.*, 44.
35. Tertullian, *De Pudicitia* 21.
36. *Testimony of Truth* 73.18–22, in NHL 415.
37. *Ibid.*, 69.9–10, in NHL 414.
38. *Ibid.*, 69.18, in NHL 414.
39. *Ibid.*, 44.30–45.4, in NHL 411. Emphasis added.
40. *Ibid.*, 69.22–24, in NHL 414.
41. *Ibid.*, 68.8–12, in NHL 414.
42. *Authoritative Teaching* 22.19 (*passim*), in NHL 278 ff.
43. *Ibid.*, 23.13–14, in NHL 279.
44. *Ibid.*, 34.19, in NHL 283.
45. *Ibid.*, 34.4, in NHL 282.
46. *Ibid.*, 34.12–13, in NHL 282.
47. *Ibid.*, 33.4–5, in NHL 282.
48. *Ibid.*, 34.20–23, in NHL 283.
49. *Ibid.*, 22.28–34, in NHL 278.
50. *Ibid.*, 34.32–35.16, in NHL 283.
51. *Ibid.*, 33.4–34.9, in NHL 282.
52. *Ibid.*, 33.16–17, in NHL 282.
53. *Ibid.*, 32.30–33.3, in NHL 282.
54. *Ibid.*, 32.30–32, in NHL 282.
55. *Ibid.*, 27.6–15, in NHL 280.
56. Tertullian, DE PRAESCR. 7.
57. *Ibid.*, 41.
58. *Ibid.*, 8–11.
59. *Ibid.*, 11.
60. Irenaeus, AH 2.27.2.
61. Clemens Alexandrinus, EXCERPTA 4.1.

Notes

62. *Ibid.*, 41.2.
63. *Ibid.*, 24.1–2.
64. Heracleon, Frag. 37–38, in Origen, COMM. JO. 13.51–13.53.
65. Irenaeus, AH 1.8.3–4.
66. Heracleon, Frag. 13, in Origen, COMM. JO. 10.33. For discussion, see E. Pagels, *The Johannine Gospel in Gnostic Exegesis* (Nashville, 1973), 66–74.
67. *Interpretation of Knowledge* 5.33, in NHL 429.
68. *Ibid.*, 6.33–38, in NHL 429.
69. For discussion, see Koschorke, *op. cit.*, 69–71; Koschorke, "Eine neugefundene gnostische Gemeindeordnung," in *Zeitschrift für Theologie und Kirche* 76.1 (February 1979), 30–60; J. Turner and E. Pagels, introduction to *Interpretation of Knowledge* (CG XI, 1) in *Nag Hammadi Studies* (Leiden, 1980).
70. I Corinthians 12:14–21.
71. *Interpretation of Knowledge* 18.28–34, in NHL 433.
72. *Ibid.*, 15.35–17.27, in NHL 432–433.
73. *Ibid.*, 18.24–25, in NHL 433.

CHAPTER SIX

1. John 14:5–6.
2. Irenaeus, AH 3.11.7. For discussion, see E. Pagels, *The Johannine Gospel in Gnostic Exegesis* (Nashville, 1973).
3. *Dialogue of the Savior* 142.16–19, in NHL 237.
4. *Gospel of Thomas* 38.4–10, in NHL 121.
5. F. Wisse, "Gnosticism and Early Monasticism in Egypt," in *Gnosis: Festschrift für Hans Jonas* (Göttingen, 1978), 431–440.
6. B. Layton, ed., *The Rediscovery of Gnosticism* (forthcoming).
7. Irenaeus, AH 4.11.2.
8. *Ibid.*, 4.11.2.
9. Justin Martyr, *Dialogue with Trypho* 4.
10. *Gospel of Philip* 71.35–72.4, in NHL 143.
11. Irenaeus, AH 1.11.1.
12. *Ibid.*, 1.12.3.
13. *Ibid.*, 1.12.3.
14. *Ibid.*, 1.12.4.
15. *Ibid.*, 1.30.6.
16. Romans 3:23.
17. Mark 1:15.
18. John 3:17–19.
19. Irenaeus, AH 1.5.4.

20. *Gospel of Truth* 17.10–16, in NHL 38.
21. *Ibid.*, 28.16–17, in NHL 42.
22. *Ibid.*, 29.2–6, in NHL 43.
23. *Ibid.*, 29.8–30.12, in NHL 43.
24. *Ibid.*, 21.35–36, in NHL 40.
25. *Ibid.*, 24.32–25.3, in NHL 41.
26. *Dialogue of the Savior* 134.1–22, in NHL 234.
27. *Gospel of Thomas* 45.30–33, in NHL 126.
28. *Ibid.*, 33.11–13, in NHL 118.
29. *Book of Thomas the Contender* 138.13, in NHL 189.
30. *Gospel of Thomas* 38.23–29, in NHL 121. For a discussion of these metaphors, see H. Jonas, *The Gnostic Religion* (Boston, 1963), 48–96, and G. MacRae, "Sleep and Awakening in Gnostic Texts," in *Le Origini dello Gnosticismo*, 496–507.
31. Professors M. L. Peel and J. Zandee have stated that the *Teachings of Silvanus* is clearly "non-Gnostic" (NHL 346). Nevertheless, what Peel and Zandee describe as characteristic of gnostic teaching (dualistic theology, docetic Christology, the doctrine that "only some persons are saved 'by nature'") does not, as they apparently assume, characterize such teaching as that of Valentinus (which undisputably *is* gnostic). The *Teachings of Silvanus* certainly is unique among the Nag Hammadi find in that most of its elements do not contradict orthodox doctrine. Whether or not it is itself a gnostic document, I suggest that what warrants its inclusion with gnostic writings is its premise that divine reason (and, apparently, divine nature) is discovered *within* oneself.
32. *Teachings of Silvanus* 88.24–92.12, in NHL 349–350.
33. *Gospel of Thomas* 32.14–19, in NHL 118.
34. *Dialogue of the Savior* 125.18–19, in NHL 231.
35. *Teachings of Silvanus* 85.24–106.14, in NHL 347–356.
36. *Ibid.*, 106.30–117.20, in NHL 356–361.
37. *Gospel of Truth* 21.11–22.15, in NHL 40.
38. *Ibid.*, 32.38–39, in NHL 44.
39. *Ibid.*, 32.31–33.14, in NHL 44.
40. *Gospel of Thomas* 32.19–33.5, in NHL 118. Emphasis added.
41. *Ibid.*, 42.7–51.18, in NHL 123–130.
42. *Ibid.*, 37.20–35, in NHL 121.
43. Mark 9:1; cf. Mark 14:62.
44. *Ibid.*, 13:5–7.
45. Luke 17:21.
46. Mark 8:27–29.
47. Matthew 16:17–18.
48. *Gospel of Thomas* 34.30–35.7, in NHL 119.
49. *Ibid.*, 50.28–30, in NHL 129.
50. *Book of Thomas the Contender* 138.13, in NHL 189.
51. *Gospel of Thomas* 48.20–25, in NHL 128.

Notes

52. *Ibid.*, 40.20–23, in NHL 122.
53. *Dialogue of the Savior* 132.15–16, in NHL 233.
54. *Ibid.*, 126.5–8, in NHL 231.
55. *Ibid.*, 140.3–4, in NHL 236.
56. *Testimony of Truth* 44.2, in NHL 410–411.
57. *Ibid.*, 43.26, in NHL 410.
58. *Ibid.*, 44.13–16, in NHL 411.
59. *Teachings of Silvanus* 97.18–98.10, in NHL 352.
60. Matthew 2:15, *passim.*
61. Justin, I *Apology* 31.
62. *Gospel of Thomas* 42.13–18, in NHL 124.
63. Irenaeus, AH 1.11.1.
64. *Ibid.*, 1.2.2.
65. *Gospel of Philip* 54.13–15, in NHL 133.
66. *Ibid.*, 67.9–12, in NHL 140.
67. *Ibid.*, 61.24–26, in NHL 137.
68. *Ibid.*, 61.29–35, in NHL 137.
69. *Ibid.*, 67.26–27, in NHL 140.
70. *Book of Thomas the Contender* 138.16–18, in NHL 189.
71. Hippolytus, REF 6.9.
72. *Ibid.*, 6.17.
73. *Gospel of Thomas* 33.14–19, in NHL 118.
74. Plotinus, "Against the Gnostics," *Enneads* 2.9.
75. *Zostrianos* 1.12, in NHL 369.
76. *Ibid.*, 2.8–9, in NHL 369.
77. *Ibid.*, 3.14–21, in NHL 370.
78. *Ibid.*, 3.29–30, in NHL 370.
79. *Ibid.*, 131.16–132.5, in NHL 393.
80. *Discourse on the Eighth and the Ninth* 52.1–7, in NHL 292.
81. *Ibid.*, 53.7–10, in NHL 293.
82. *Ibid.*, 52.15–18, in NHL 293.
83. *Ibid.*, 54.23–25, in NHL 293.
84. *Ibid.*, 56.10–12, in NHL 294.
85. *Ibid.*, 56.17–22, in NHL 294.
86. *Ibid.*, 57.3–11, in NHL 294.
87. *Ibid.*, 57.31–58.22, in NHL 295.
88. *Ibid.*, 58.31–61.2, in NHL 295–296.
89. *Ibid.*, 63.9–14, in NHL 297.
90. *Allogenes* 52.8–12, in NHL 446.
91. *Ibid.*, 50.19, in NHL 445.
92. *Ibid.*, 52.15–21, in NHL 446.
93. *Ibid.*, 53.36–37, in NHL 447.
94. *Ibid.*, 55.31–57.34, in NHL 447–448.
95. *Ibid.*, 59.9–37, in NHL 449.
96. *Ibid.*, 60.13–18, in NHL 449.

97. *Ibid.*, 60.37–61.8, in NHL 449.

98. *Ibid.*, 61.14–16, in NHL 449–450.

99. *Ibid.*, 61.29–31, in NHL 450.

100. *Ibid.*, 64.16–23, in NHL 451.

101. *Ibid.*, 67.23–35, in NHL 451–452.

102. *Ibid.*, 68.18–19.

103. Tertullian, *Adversus Valentinianos* 1.

CONCLUSION

1. Tertullian, DE PRAESCR. 13.

2. *Gospel of Truth* 17.10–11, in NHL 38.

3. Irenaeus, AH 1.5.4.

4. *Gospel of Truth* 16.1–18.34, in NHL 37–38.

5. Plotinus, "Against the Gnostics," *Enneads* 2.9.

6. A. D. Nock, "Gnosticism," in *Arthur Darby Nock: Essays on Religion and the Ancient World*, ed. Z. Stewart (Cambridge, 1972), Vol. 2, 943.

7. Nock, "Gnosticism," 942.

8. *Gospel of Thomas* 41.27–30, in NHL 123.

9. Heracleon, Frag. 39, in Origen, COMM. JO. 13.53.

10. *Gospel of Thomas* 42.16–18, in NHL 124.

11. *Testimony of Truth* 68.8–12, in NHL 414.

12. Irenaeus, AH 2.22.4.

13. *Ibid.*, 2.22.5–6.

14. *Gospel of Thomas* 38.1–3, in NHL 121.

15. H. Koester, "The Structure of Early Christian Beliefs," in *Trajectories Through Early Christianity* (Philadelphia, 1971), 231.

16. Irenaeus, AH 1.10.2.

17. Luke 14:26.

18. Mark 4:10–12, *par.*

19. Matthew 19:4–6, *par.*

20. *Ibid.*, 19:13–15, *par.*

21. Mark 1:41, 3:3–5, *par.*

22. Luke 19:41–44.

23. W. Blake, "The Everlasting Gospel," 2a and g.

24. F. Nietzsche, *The Antichrist.*

25. F. Dostoevsky, "The Grand Inquisitor," in *The Brothers Karamazov.*

26. *Second Treatise of the Great Seth* 61.20, in NHL 334.

27. A. D. Nock, "The Study of the History of Religion," in *Arthur Darby Nock*, Vol. 1, 339.

INDEX

Since receiving her doctorate from Harvard University in 1970, ELAINE PAGELS has taught at Barnard College, Columbia University. She has chaired the department of religion at Barnard since 1975. Besides participating with other scholars in editing several of the texts from Nag Hammadi, Professor Pagels is the author of two previous books, *The Johannine Gospel in Gnostic Exegesis* and *The Gnostic Paul: Gnostic Exegesis of the Pauline Letters*. She and her husband live in New York City.